The Secret Of Bhagavad Gita

Discover The World's Grandest Truth

Sri Vishwanath

www.secretofbhagavadgita.com

ISBN: 978-0-9817703-9-0

Published by Soul Power Magic (owned by the author himself Anantharaman Vishwanath)

You can contact the author at free109@gmail.com**. You can also reach him at his USA number at 2138142680. India contact number 91-22-21645009.**

Also by Sri Vishwanath

1) **Shakti** : The Greatest Secret To A Stress Free Life.

2) **No-Nonsense Meditation**: What The Greatest Wise Men & Women Knew About Human Consciousness That You Are Not Aware Of.

3) **The Joy of Becoming God.**

4) **The Power Of The Vedas:** The Spiritual Guide That Has Been 5500 Years In The Making.

5) **The Story of Nachiketa**

6) **Seven Spiritual Strategies**- How The Enlightenment Code Can Change Your Life

7) **Give Up Your Excess Baggage:** 24 Simple Mind Exercises That Great Men & Women Effectively Use Every Single Day.

8) **Shiva:** Four Ancient Secrets To Win God's Grace.

9) **Zero Effort**: Maximising Potential With Ease.

Dedication

TO LORD KRISHNA,
SRI RAMAKRISHNA, SWAMI VIVEKANANDA,
SRI SHARADA DEVI, Sri Ramana Maharishi,
Jagadguru Shankaracharya Sri Sri Bharati Tirtha
Mahaswamiji of Sringeri,
Goddess Kali, Sree Manappully Bhagavathy Devi

Acknowledgments

To Dr A .G. Krishna Warrier , author of *Srimad Bhagavad Gita Bhasya* , published by the Ramakrishna Math. His translations of each (sloka) from Sanskrit to English is the best I have ever come across.

To Jack Adler for his flawless editing and untiring patience in removing the weeds out of my book.

To John Harricharan for writing the foreword to the book.

To Satyanarayan Pandey of Mumbai for all administrative guidance.

To my father and mother for instilling the spiritual culture. I am forever grateful for that.

To my wife for allowing my spiritual side to blossom and for being patient with my spiritual outbursts. I want to thank her from the bottom of my heart.

To my son Vignesh whose birth changed the very course of my life.

To Lord Krishna for choosing me to help readers fully understand and appreciate this wonderful epic.

Table Of Contents

Foreword

By John Harricharan

(Award Winning Author of "When You Can Walk On Water Take The Boat" and many other bestsellers)

When Sri Vishwanath asked me if I would write the foreword for his new book, "The Secret of the Bhagavad Gita," I thought to myself, "Not another book about the subtleties of ancient, holy books!" You see, I was born into a Hindu family, became a Christian, lived and learned from Muslims, Hindus, Christians, Jews, Sikhs and members of different religions.

At an early age, I had read many of the scriptures of different religions. I had learned about the Ramayana and the Bhagavad Gita from my father, mother and family. I had read the Christian Bible three times by the age of ten or eleven and was somewhat familiar with Islam and its teachings, as well as with the Jewish Torah.

Needless to say, I was fascinated by all these religious texts. I found "truths" expressed in different ways and I discovered that all mankind and their religions had much more in common than I had imagined. It seemed as if the ancient sages, rishis and prophets were all trying to tell us the same thing in different ways.

Yet, there were difficulties in understanding many areas of the various works. Each religion, and each holy book contained so much wisdom and guidance that we may find ourselves caught up in the complexities and interpretations of various stories or teachings.

And so it was that I started to read Sri Vishwanath's manuscript called, "The Secret of the Bhagavad Gita." At first, I just thought that I'd glance through it, get the general idea and continue with my other tasks. I was always familiar with parts of the conversation between Krishna and Arjuna as they stood between the two mighty armies that were ready to go into mortal combat.

Yet, I could not put the manuscript down until I had read the last word. Vishwanath brings great clarity to a seemingly complex work. He uses many fine examples as he drills down into the heart of the Bhagavad Gita in seeking its truths and guidance. Only a seasoned and wise author and teacher could find the hidden secrets.

Had it been only an academic explanation of the Bhagavad Gita, that in itself would have surely been enough. But he provides simple exercises to give us deeper insights, which provide us with practical means to solve many of our problems. What I also found very refreshing was Vish's respect and reverence for other religions and faiths. There was tremendous understanding and no judgment. He did not attack nor defend any one faith. He just gives the reader what he found and leaves it up to us to do what we want with it. This, in my view, is awesome!

I have to remember that all religions point us in the direction of "Truth." I am also reminded that we must never confuse the pointer with the way itself. Perhaps, in your reading of this fantastic book, you may find some things that you would want to question. That is fine. Questions are always good. But you will also find many thoughts that resonate with your deepest feelings. It's like attending a great feast. You don't have to eat everything you see. You may not like everything, but you'll surely find enough to fill your hunger.

Follow Vishwanath on this adventure and watch your life change from mediocrity to excellence. You, too, will discover what Albert Einstein, Albert Schweitzer, Carl Jung, Aurobindo, Thoreau, Gandhi, Emerson, and countless others discovered in the Bhagavad Gita. Thank you, Sri Vishwanath, thank you for revealing to us the Secret of the Bhagavad Gita.

Preface

*You may be the greatest philosopher but as long
as you have the idea that you are the body, you are no
better than the little worm crawling under your foot! No
excuse for you! So much the worse for you, that you know
all the philosophies and at the same time think you are
the body! Body-gods that is what you are! Is that religion?*

Swami Vivekananda

The *Bhagavad Gita* , which means "Song Of God"
in English, requires a little preliminary introduction. The
scene is set in the battlefield of Kurukshetra where two
opponents of the same race fight for the empire of India.
The Pandavas stood for righteousness and the Kauravas
for dominance. The Pandavas were five brothers who had
the right to the throne but were forced to leave the
kingdom and move into the forest for 13 years after
losing a game of dice to the Kauravas. At the end of the
13 year period, when the Pandavas returned, the
Kauravas would not grant them back their share of the
kingdom.

The deity, Krishna, was a friend of the Pandavas
and he agreed to be the charioteer and advisor for
Arjuna who was one of the five Pandavas and the
sharpest bowman among all the warriors.

The opening scene of *Bhagavad Gita* is on the
battlefield of Kurukshetra where both sides can see their
relatives and friends ...one brother on one side and
another on the other flank, a grandfather on one side
and a grandson on another.

The *Bhagavad Gita* begins with Arjuna saying to Krishna, "Station the chariot, O Krishna !, between the two armies that I may behold my opponents with whom I have to fight."

Krishna blew the Pancajanya, the divine conch, and stationed the large chariot yoked with white steeds in between the two armies. Arjuna saw many family members in the ranks of the two armies-fathers, grandfathers, teachers, uncles, brothers, sons, grandson as well as father inlaws and friends.

Thus began confusion in Arjuna's mind.

Arjuna tells Krishna: "My limbs droop, my mouth dries up, my body trembles, and my bow slips from my grip. I don't seek victory, O Krishna. I want neither kingdom nor pleasures. What pleasure shall be ours by killing my own friends and relatives?"

Throwing away his bow and arrows while his mind was consumed with grief Arjuna sank into the seat of the chariot. The dialogue between Krishna and Arjuna that ensued next is one of the most famous discussions in religious literature.

Krishna replies : "From whence has this timidity, unwelcome to noble spirits, unheavenly and disgraceful come upon you in such a crisis? Yield not to unmanliness, O Arjuna. It does not befit thee. It is unbecoming of you."

Krishna is sharp to the point and he sees through the conflict in Arjuna's heart -- the conflict between his emotionalism and his duty. "You grieve, O Arjuna, for those who call for no grief, at the same time you utter words of wisdom. It is unbecoming of you. The wise grieves neither for the dead nor for the living."

The word **"unbecoming"** is the seed on which the entire teaching of Krishna in the *Bhagavad Gita* is based. Krishna then delivers even more truths to Arjuna, dispelling all the myths and false beliefs that keep him from realizing his true nature. With his confusion dispelled and memory of truth regained Arjuna goes on achieve victory in the historic war.

This book isn't a commentary on the entire sermon delivered by Krishna to Arjuna. The focus is on revealing the essence of *Bhagavad Gita*, the secret yoga of Krishna , and the unseen laws of the other worlds.

Krishna tells Arjuna: "Whosoever studies this righteous dialogue between us shall will be liberated and will reach the happy realms reserved for the meritorious."

Chapter 1

God is not a belief. He is the highest law which runs this universe.

Says Krishna to Arjuna: "Of creation I am the beginning, the middle ,and the end. Of the sciences I am the science of the self. Of those who discuss I am the dialectic."

What is the proof of God?

It is direct perception, explains Krishna. Pratyaksha is the Sanskrit word for direct perception. How do we perceive the wall in our house? Through our senses. We can see the wall and touch it and so we conclude that the wall exists. If we stretch our intellect a little further and inquire about the source of the wall we can find the builder who constructed the wall. If we allow our mind to explore even further in this direction we can discover the architect of this universe.

Krishna continues: "Of the luminaries I am the sun, of the stars I am the moon, of the senses I am the mind, of the secrets I am the silence, of the learned I am the knowledge, of all beings I am the intelligence."

Imagine the following scene before you. You look out of the window and you see an apple falling from the tree for the first time in your life. You get excited and wonder how could this apple fall to the ground. Next day you again look out of the window and observe another apple falling to the ground. You're now convinced that most apples will fall to the ground and you bring your family and friends the following day to the yard. Pointing to an apple on the tree you say, "I believe this apple will fall to the ground in the next few minutes."

Does your belief has anything to do with the apple falling to the ground? The apple falls to the ground because of the law of gravity. Does a scientist ever say, "I believe the apple will fall to the ground?" The scientist declares: "The apple falls to the ground because of the law of gravity."

Beliefs and laws are two separate things. **You tend to believe many things until the time that the law isn't completely known to you**. Once the law is known there is no more belief.

God is not a belief. He stands for the highest law which runs this universe.

The Higher Laws of the Universe

"The demoniac thinks that the world is ungrounded and born of mutual union but the wise knows it otherwise," Krishna advises Arjuna.

Science has discovered many natural laws after observing, studying, and interpreting the workings of the universe. Simplistic however , there have been wise beings in the past and in the present day too who haven't gone to school and yet they have understood the world through selfless love, flawless purity ,they have mastery of the law of giving. Aware of higher laws in existence superior to the ordinary workings of the human mind they had the courage and determination to pursue them.

How laws became a belief is a fascinating study.

When Krishna, Christ, Buddha, Mohammed and the founders of other religions spoke about these higher laws they had to use examples and stories to convey the essence of these tenets. These written words soon became subject to interpretation and as time progressed developed into a belief system. This variation in such beliefs is the result of much of the conflict in the world. The spiritual books and the symbols which these great men left behind were expressions of these higher laws.

Truth is never in the arrangement of the words. The law is the truth.

Everything else is an expression of these laws and subject to human interpretation. All the great scriptures can appear to be different when you pay more attention to the choice of words used in these writings rather than strive to discover the higher laws which they were meant to express.

Unity can only be found in the law.

If spiritual laws are known, practised and perfected by every being there would be better appreciation for all religions, more respect and love for one another , and peace in this world.

Chapter 2

The field and the knower of the field
Spiritual Law No 1

Says Krishna to Arjuna: "All beings in this world, moving and non-moving , are born out of the union of Purusha (self) and Prakarti (catalyst of change). He who knows the Purusha and the Prakarti is no longer born in this world ,no matter how he or she fares in this world."

What is Prakarti and Purusha?

This is how Krishna explains these concepts to Arjuna: "Know Prakarti to be the field, the changes in the field, and the agents of change. Know Purusha to be me- the knower of the field."

What ,then, is the field? The field is your body, your mind, and the whole of nature.

The changes in the field are the effects of your thoughts and action. Every thought or action produces either pain or pleasure. These are the changes in the field.

The agents of change are the three constituents which force the change to happen in the field.

Krishna says all the changes happening within you and in nature are because of the agents of change.

You feel happy, you feel sad, you get angry, you get attracted towards something, you get old and you die. Summer changes to winter, seed grows into a fruit, water turns to water vapour. All changes without exception come because of the three agents of change operating in the field. These three agents of change are the root cause for the glaring differences in human personalities.

The Three Agents of Change

No 1: Agent of error (Tamasic) – This agent forces you to view the part as the whole. Here's an example. One who enjoys eating apples will talk about it as if it was the only fruit existing on earth.

No 2: Agent of equal opportunity (Rajasic) – This agent forces you to respect and accept the individual existence of everything. One who enjoys eating an apple will also accept that a mango, banana, orange and every other fruit existing on earth has a justified existence.

No 3: Agent of oneness (Sattvic) – This agent forces you to discover unity in diversity. All fruits apple, mango, banana orange and every other fruit comes from the seed which is created by God.

"I am the seed of all beings ," Krishna tells Arjuna. "That which is without me, mobile or stationery exists not."

These three agents of change exist in varying proportions in every being. They force one to think and act in a particular way resulting in mutual conflict and disharmony in the world. Krishna says a wicked person is one who is largely influenced by the agent of error operating within his being. A wealthy and respected person is one who is highly influenced by the agent of equal opportunity existing within him or herself. A wise person is one in whom the agent of oneness dominates.

In essence, Krishna explains that you're not the agent of change.

Wickedness, richness, respect, and knowledge are all elements triggered by the agent of change. You think cruel and you become wicked over time. You work hard and you gain fame and wealth in the future. You spend time in silence and you're rewarded with an increase in your power of observation. In this regard, Krishna says: "That which makes you think cruelly is the agent of error operating within you. That which forces you to work hard to accomplish your goals is the agent of equal opportunity in you. That which urges you to spend time in silence is the agent of oneness within you. Your personality is made up of what you think and act but your thoughts and action are driven by the agent of change operating within you."

Krishna advises to never ask the question "How can I change my attitude? How can I get rid of my anger? How can I overcome procrastination, and how can I be more loving and caring towards others? Instead, Krishna says you don't need to change, overcome , or get rid of anything. You simply need to identify the agent of change operating within you and learn to disassociate yourself from it. The moment you do that you would no longer be bound by the qualities of that agent.

The field, the changes in the field, and the agents of change together form Prakarti. You are not the Prakarti , says Krishna. "You are not the body, you are not the mind, you are not the changes happening in the body and the mind. You are the Purusha. You are the self and you are the non-agent."

"He alone sees who sees on all sides all actions performed by Prakarti and the Self as the non-agent," Krishna declares.

Imagine there is a fire burning and you put your hand in it and you say it is hot. The fire burning is Prakarti and if you put your hand in it will burn. Take your hand out knowing that you are not the fire and you need not experience the heat of the fire. You are the Purusha , the soul and the spirit.

Krishna's point is that creation is a combination of two things: Something that is subject to change and something that isn't subject to change. That which is subject to change is Prakarti and that which isn't subject to change is Purusha. Creation happens when Purusha and Prakarti unite. Take anything in this world and there is something which gets destroyed over time and there is something which prevails over eternity. Prakarti only appears to have an independent existence when you relate to the agents of change; however , the moment you break free from these agents of change you discover Prakarti to be united in the Purusha.

"He alone sees who sees the multiplicity of beings as abiding in one and the plurality of beings as proceeding from that one self," Krishna says.

"You are the self," Krishna asserts. "You are complete. You can't be destroyed. You can't be influenced. What can't be completed, destroyed, or influenced is Prakarti. Hold on to the Purusha and break free from the Prakarti at this moment. Know that the whole of nature is for the soul and not the soul for the nature."

How To Break Free From Prakarti?

1) Feel happy realising:-You are not your thoughts.

You might have heard this a million times: You are not your thoughts. But did that make you feel happy or was that just a philosophical thought. Here's an example which will help you get this right.

Imagine the following scene. You have to brush your teeth tomorrow morning. The whole day you keep thinking: "I have to brush my teeth."

" I have to brush my teeth..."

" I have to brush my teeth..."

Let's take this one step further. You now stick a note to yourself in your bathroom and paste it on all corners of your room. Look how ridiculous it seems.

All that was needed was for you to get up in the morning and have one single thought of brushing your teeth. You would then simply go and brush your teeth. **Thinking isn't a necessity. You have to think only when you need to get something done.**

"Of the secrets I am the silence, " Krishna says, continuing his discourse with Arjuna.

Silence isn't the absence of thoughts. Neither is it about keeping quiet. Silence is a state of being where you think only when it is necessary.

The Vedas, one of the oldest Hindu scripture

declares "The mind of a fool is caught in thinking or not thinking but the wise man is of the nature of no thought for he or she thinks only what is appropriate."

A still mind is man's greatest asset. When your mind is alert you identify yourself with the Purusha (the self) and experience great strength. When your mind is weighed down by thoughts , your identification leans towards the thoughts and you drift in the cycle of pain and pleasure.

Thoughts become powerful when you choose to create them.

Thoughts drain away your energy when you allow your circumstances to influence your thoughts.

Never forget :You are responsible for your thoughts but you are not your thoughts.

You can choose to still your mind at any point of time. It is Prakarti which influences you to relate to the thoughts. Thoughts drain away your energy. Think only when it's necessary. Feel relieved that you're not your thoughts and that you have the freedom to create them when necessary.

2) Feel happy knowing : You are not your experiences.

"Purusha lodged in Prakarti experiences the constituents born of Prakarti, Krishna informs Arjuna. The cause of birth in the womb, good or evil , arises as a result of holding on to the three agents of change."

Krishna repeatedly says that the root cause of all pain and pleasure in this universe is caused as a result of associating with the three agents of change. Therefore, he advises Arjuna to break free from these agents of change.

The Purusha never participates in experiences but it only observes. That which participates in experiences is Prakarti. When Purusha is united with Prakarti it appears that Purusha is experiencing the pain and pleasure however that is not true. Think about it. **What will happen to your personality if all your previous experiences are taken away from you?** Would there be any aspect of your personality which will exist if all your previous experiences are destroyed? It's this aspect of your personality that represents your real nature and what's worthy to be known. Everything else is subject to change.

Let me walk you through an example.

Believe you have three suits or dresses to wear. One of them is completely soiled, the other is torn, and the third one is neat, clean and ironed. Which one will you pick up? It goes without saying that you will choose the one which is neat and clean.

This means you have the ability to choose or identify that thing which is best for you. You simply made the choice for the cleanest outfit. All the three outfits were yours you acknowledged it you did not disown it you simply made the choice for the cleanest one.

You have to do the same thing with your experiences. You're not your experience just like you're not the dress or suit. You observed the outfit and so you were able to choose the best one. **Similarly, you have to train yourself to *observe* your past experiences and not rush to relate yourself to them**. Observe all your experiences, both good and bad ,with a calm mind. There's nothing to get excited about if you had a great experience and nothing to feel dejected over if you had a painful one. All your past experiences represent that aspect of your personality that's subject to change. Whether the outfit in the above example is soiled or clean really doesn't matter. You're not your experiences. If relating to a previous experience makes you feel happy and increases your self worth , by all means do it. You have the power to choose from a previous experience. Be bold enough to observe and choose. That which observes is Purusha and that which chooses and experiences is Prakarti.

There is only one sin in this world," Krishna declares. "Thinking about sin is the greatest sin."

You're not your past thoughts. You're not your past experiences. You have the freedom to create a brand new experience. Be bold in dumping dull and lazy thoughts as well as painful and guilty ones. You are the Purusha and you are complete. Experiences and thoughts can never create a dent in you if you don't relate to the three agents of change.

3) Feel confident in meditating: You are not your current circumstances.

Once you fully realize that you're not your thoughts and not your experiences, what follows logically is that you're not your current circumstances either.

Your present situation only reveals your personality which is a direct reflection of your current thoughts at this time. If you're going through a bad situation your thoughts would be low and dejected. No matter what you do it will remain the same. You need powerful thoughts and abundant energy to change your current circumstance and there's only one proven way to achieve that. You have to train yourself to disassociate thoughts from what makes you feel incomplete and relate to that aspect within you which is complete. The moment you do that you will start feeling good and everything else will fall in place.

Here's another example. Let's say that you're broke and want to become self sufficient . So there are two aspects of your personality. One in which you're broke and the other a personality where you have abundant money. Now ask yourself "Do you think you deserve to be abundant? Do you want to enjoy an abundant personality that's full of life and purpose and ready to take on life's challenges."

Of course, most of us would strive for the abundant personality.

"You can only become something which you are," Krishna explains. "You can never become something which you are not."

Love, compassion, purity, abundance are the higher aspects of your personality. Confusion, indecision, scarcity and stress are the lower aspects of your personality. Krishna says the easiest way to change your circumstances is to disassociate yourself from the agent of error and associate yourself with the agent of oneness and equal opportunity. The moment you make this switch your thoughts and action will drive you towards abundance, love , and compassion.

What makes you feel broke are your thoughts , experiences , and current circumstances which are influenced largely by the agent of error operating within you. Break free, and simply feel happy that you're not your current circumstance. Sit in a quiet place and get in touch with that thing which isn't your thoughts about your experiences and your current circumstance. Out of this meditation will come power, peace ,goodness, and everything that you aspire for.

4) Feel strong in your realization that : You can get in touch with your real nature right now.

" An eternal part of my being has become the Jiva in all beings," Krishna relates. "It pulls the five senses together and the mind as the sixth that are set in Prakarti. All beings dwell in me but I dwell not in them"

Krishna says just as the one sun illumines the entire world so the owner of the field illumines the entire field by becoming the "jiva" in every being. Jiva stands for the individual soul present in all beings, that aspect of your personality which can never be destroyed or influenced by anything. We will cover this aspect in great detail in the next chapter.

Arjuna asks an important question to Krishna here. "If all the changes happening in the universe are caused as a result of the three agents of change operating in the field , then what is the ultimate goal of human life?"

And the answer comes: "He who perseveres

embued with yoga sees the jiva (soul) dwelling in the inner self while those of unpurified mind , not having mastered their inner self , fail to see me despite perseverance."

This is a beautiful message from Krishna ,who says the goal of human life is to find unity. His message is clearly that enthusiasm and determination won't help you reach the goal ; it only helps you pursue the goal. To reach the goal of unity you need to be embued with yoga.

Yoga doesn't mean sitting or standing and twisting your hand and body. The reference to yoga here is something else. It's about transcending your association with the three agents of change which we discussed earlier. Those who fail to master this yoga won't find him, Krishna predicts; but he who perseveres and strives to master this yoga will unite with him.

In a divine promise, Krishna says: "To the single minded Yogin in perpetual communion with me I am always easily accessible."

Prakarti
(The cause which accomplishes all effects)
The agents of change

Three Agents of change	Qualities of the agents
Agent of Error(Tamasic)	Wickedness, procrastination & dullness
Agent of Equal opportunity(Rajasic)	Seeking wealth and power
Agent of Oneness(Satvic)	Seeking unity in diversity

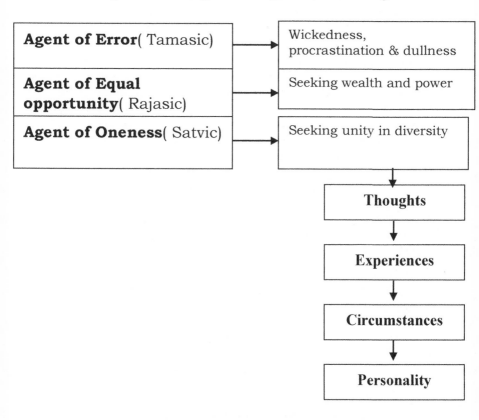

Thoughts

↓

Experiences

↓

Circumstances

↓

Personality

You are not the Prakarti. You are not your thoughts experiences and circumstances.

You are not the three agents of change. You are the Purusha.

Krishna's winning formula to develop the right attitude

Do this exercise when fresh and full of energy. Close your eyes and imagine that you're in New York and you have to travel to Washington D.C.. Heading towards the airport to catch the morning commuter flight you get an emergency phone call from Los Angeles that your father is critically ill and needs you by his side. You cancel your trip to Washington D.C. and instead fly to Los Angeles city. In LA a series of quick events follow as you take care of your father. You get a new job opportunity; you meet the love of your life ; and very soon you've found a new home in Los Angeles city.

Two decades pass by in Los Angeles. You go through many other exciting and painful experiences in your life. Life continues until one day a childhood friend from New York turns up at your apartment. You spend a great time together catching up on past memories. As he bids you goodbye he poses an interesting question:

"I enjoyed listening to all your exciting experiences in LA and I'm proud of how you overcame the painful ones. My gut however tells me that your goal is still in Washington."

Now open your eyes, take a brand new notepad , and write these five sentences

1) **Goals and experiences are two different things**. Every experience is valid and helps to shape up my personality. However, if my goal is to be in Washington, then all my experiences in Los Angeles -- no matter how exciting they may seem to be – wouldn't really matter in the end.

2) **The battlefield is more important than the battle**. There is victory and defeat in every battle. However, if I'm fighting in a wrong battlefield my triumph or loss really doesn't matter.

3) **Purusha is the goal** . That battlefield which helps me remember Purusha is the ideal one.

4) **Manage the battle correctly**. My thoughts about my experiences and current circumstances are the battle I wage in my mind. This battle appears to be complicated when I lose sight of the Purusha but becomes quite manageable when I remember the goal of Purusha.

5) **Remember Purusha**. When I forget the goal and the battlefield I get caught in the battle. When I remember Purusha I rise above Prakarti.

■■

Krishna counsels Arjuna to: "Always remember me and fight . Fix your mind and intellect on me. Rid of all doubts you will surely attain me for you are dear to me."

Chapter 3

The Secret Yoga of Krishna and His Idea of Heaven

Spiritual Law No 2

What happens after death?

This question has been answered by many wise beings in the past. But this is how Krishna reveals the law of life after death. The question of "what happens after death" is never a mystery. It's a law , says Krishna , and this axiom can be known. However, the mechanics of this precept and the finer details which makes this law work will forever remain a mystery. Krishna urges us to know the law first rather than worry about its operation. The law of death doesn't differentiate between the death of an atheist, an agnostic , a Hindu, a Muslim , a Christian , a Buddhist , or any other religion. The rule of death treats all of them the same.

The Law of Life After Death

First Krishna explains: "Having enjoyed the vast world of heaven, the merits spent, one enters into the world of mortals. Guided by the intelligence of the supreme and seeking pleasure in objects one attains movement to and from heaven."

What is heaven? You'll be shocked to know that heaven isn't the final destination for the soul. Heaven is like a sojourn. It's a brief period of rest for the soul after which it returns back to earth. There are worlds much superior to heaven , says Krishna.

The Four Parallel Worlds

There are four parallel worlds in existence at any point of time. The first is the earth world where we human beings live.

1) **Earth sphere**- In the earth world force is physical and matter is sensible. Everything in this universe from human beings to plants , to animals, and natural objects   exist as a combination of force and matter. Force and matter can be easily differentiated on earth. Force can be physically felt and matter is very much visible. Take the example of a table fan. When the table fan isn't operated you only see the blades of the fan. However , when you switch on the fan the blades start moving and becomes invisible, the air becomes cooler , and you experience the manifestation of force.

Your body is like the table fan and the thoughts are the force what sets you into motion. All action, inaction, knowledge ignorance, righteousness and non-righteousness exists in this world as a result of the vibration of your mind , says Krishna. When your mind is at a low vibration most of your thoughts are centered around bodily enjoyment. Your thoughts are instinctive. When this vibration of mind increases your thoughts move away from the senses and cling to the intellect.

Your thoughts are now based on the power of reasoning.

When you step up this vibration of your mind further you break free from the intellect and move beyond the body and mind into the world of super consciousness.

Your thoughts are now based on the power of inspiration.

All the pain and suffering in this world is simply because of the lack of ability to step up the vibration of your mind , says Krishna. The moment you step up the vibration of your mind you break free from the three agents of change. All those problems which seemed to haunt you earlier would no longer exist as they cease to be present at the higher level of vibration.

Here's an example. Let's say you take butter in a pan and heat it. What happens? Very quickly the butter turns to thin liquid. It has changed its form.

How did that happen? Science will tell you that the heat of the fire was the force which brought about the change. However , the same butter when it was refrigerated was solid. So what do you understand here?

The environment you place your mind in becomes a very critical factor in shaping your reality of the world.

If your mind is in a frozen state where you have identified yourself with your past experiences and thoughts you would continue to carry the same identification and your reality will be shaped by the nature of your thoughts and experiences. However, if you decide to hold on to a far superior identification of yourself you should be prepared to step up the vibration of your mind and thus influence your reality.

Heating was the catalyst of change which manifested thin liquid out of solid butter. The same thing happens when you bring all the best energy within you and throw this concentrated energy toward your desired object. The level of vibration increases. This is the key which everyone misses.

When you increase the level of vibration of your mind your power of observation goes up automatically. And when your power of observation heightens your sense of awareness also increases. This development allows to develop the power to trace the root of any problem or come up with creative solutions for the problem at hand.

When you increase the level of vibration of your mind the mind loses its identification towards those objects which existed earlier at the lower level of vibration. It then positions its identification towards those objects which exist now at the higher level of vibration.

The butter identification is gone and the liquid identification has materialized. **Vibration determines your identification and any change of vibration is what is called heightened awareness.**

When you take this to the extreme and the mind vibrates at a very high level - and by mind I mean the force which makes the mind vibrate - we enter into the second parallel world called the lunar sphere.

Lunar Sphere (The world of heaven)

"Smoke, night, dark fortnight, the six months of the sun's southern course passing in time marked by these one reaches the lunar sphere and returns back to earth," Krishna tells Arjuna.

Lunar sphere is also called the world of heaven. Lunar sphere isn't the moon as the name lunar implies. The lunar sphere surrounds and influences the workings of the earth and the entire solar system. In this world force is psychic and matter is fine. In the earth world we observed that force was physical and matter was sensible.

The lunar sphere is inhabited by gods or what in other religions are called angels. Gods , mean beings endowed with supernatural powers not common among human beings. So we have the rain god, the fire god, the water god, the god of death, the god of wealth, the god of love, the god of health , and the list goes on. These gods govern the workings of the earth world. They have psychic powers. They can fly in air, walk in water, make an elephant pass through a needle, cure any ailment,etc. These gods are limited to the powers they are allotted. So a fire god can't play with water. His powers are limited to the element of fire.

One year in the lunar sphere is equal to 360 years in the earth sphere. You might wonder how could that be possible? Let's take an example. If you're located in London and want to travel to New York , how much time would it take?

If you travel by plane you can reach New York physically in 8 hours. However , you can also reach New York in less than three seconds through your mind. You can simply close your eyes and imagine that you're in New York. The important thing to understand here is that there are physical and mental worlds within each of us. When you reach New York by plane you're travelling by the physical world and you get a valid experience. When you reach New York by mind you're travelling by the mental world and you still get a valid experience. Both the physical and mental worlds produce experiences and it's only through discrimination that we value one over another.

Eight hours in the physical world = two seconds in the mental world.

So understand that there are many parallel worlds and what takes one year in the physical world could take just one second in another world. It is very much possible.

In the psychic world - the world of gods - you can be present anywhere, and any time. Gods can travel from London to New York in less than two seconds. They have super powers as they're not limited to the workings of the body and the mind. When these gods take human forms they can even create palaces out of a blade of grass. They can create anything using solar energy.

So the lunar sphere surrounds the earth sphere and governs certain critical functions of the earth sphere.

When you die there are two paths which open up for you. Through the first you merge with the supreme. Through the second you enter into the lunar sphere (the world of heaven) and return back.

Let's talk about the second path which transports

you to the lunar sphere. Says Krishna: "Devoid of delusion and ego, overcoming the flaws of attachment, firm in spirituality, free of lust, released from the dualities of pain and pleasure one attains to the supreme."

Don't waste your time inquiring about why God created the world and inflicted so much sorrow and misery in it, Krishna advises Arjuna. He says this question is born out of ignorance , arising out of the low vibration of your mind. There are three rules of the game and if you attempt to understand and work with them you'll be able to merge with the supreme and never return back to earth. If you miss you go to the lunar sphere and return back to earth.

The rules of the game of life.

The three most important rules of the game are:
1. Everyone has to play the game of life. There are no exceptions.
2.   If you play the game you will get lost in it.
3. The one who plays the game and who doesn't get identified with the test involved wins the mortal contest.

So how do you play this game of life?

Rule 3 says "The one who plays the game and who doesn't get identified with the game wins the game"

However Rule 2 says " If you play the game you'll get lost in the game.

So how do you play the game and not get lost in it?

Rule 1 says: "Everyone has to play the game .. There is no exception. You can't quit the game.

"Purusha lodged in Prakarti experiences the constituents born of Prakarti. The cause of birth in the womb whether good or evil, arises due to holding on to the constituents of change."

Krishna maintains that you come back again and again to the earth because of your ignorance of holding on to the three agents of change. These agents of change trigger our identification with objects and facilitate our movement to and from heaven.

When you step up the vibration of your mind you lose identification with the agents of change and hold on to the supreme self.
All movements in the earth world and even in the lunar sphere are facilitated by the agents of change, Krishna explains. It's interesting to note that even in the lunar sphere the gods aren't free from the three constituents. They have superior powers but they too are attached to their powers.

As a key point, Krishna repeats to Arjuna: "No beings in this world or in the world of heaven exists who are free from the three agents of change."

Those beings who play the game of life, and learn to transcend the three agents of change , merge with the supreme. The rest when they die are transported to the lunar sphere , and after a brief period of rest return back to earth.

In defining himself, Krishna says "Of the gods I am Indra, of the Vedas I am the Sama Veda , of the subduers I am Yama."

The god of lunar sphere is called Indra which isn't the name of a person but the name given to one in charge of heaven. You may be surprised that even Indra, the god of lunar sphere , is lustful and chases women. The gods too crave for power and fight among themselves. The gods too are promoted and demoted. The god who heads the lunar sphere today could be born as a son of sweeper in the earth world tomorrow. It's quite possible, says Krishna. It all depends on your karma. Karma means actions which can nullify or offset your past actions. The gods too die. In heaven too there is death.

So the gods too have all the desires which human beings have and must go through the process of birth and death. The only difference is they play the game at a higher level due to not being restricted to the limitations of the mind and the body. So the lunar sphere, also called heaven , is only a more refined version of the earth.

Note that in the lunar sphere you don't get a chance to create fresh karma. Karma means actions which can nullify or offset your past actions. It's only in the earthly life that a murderer can become a saint. This is the reason earth life is so important and one of the factors why we return back to earth. The lunar sphere is all about enjoying the fruits of your worldly action. **You can't create fresh karma in heaven.** It's all enjoyment there. The opportunity to attain perfection is only available in the earth world. In no other worlds do you get this opportunity to attain perfection. Hence, earth life is very important and precious. It is here where you get an opportunity to achieve everything.

Human beings on earth are superior to the gods and angels.

The gods in heaven are not perfected souls. They only appear to be superior to human beings because they possess supernatural powers and are allotted roles to govern the workings of the earth world. Perfection can't be attained in heaven. Even gods and angels have to take human birth to attain perfection and thus to go beyond the lunar sphere.

Says Krishna: "The worshippers of gods proceed to gods, the worshippers of ancestors proceed to ancestors, the worshippers of elementals proceed to elementals , and my devotees come to me"

The word "gods" doesn't mean Krishna. It means the god of wealth, the god of health, the god of love , and so on. Human beings on earth who worship the god of wealth, the god of health, the god of love, and the god of removing obstacles can reach the lunar sphere. They attain to heaven, and have to return back to earth after a brief period of enjoyment. It would be interesting to note that the gods of heaven can influence the workings of the earth and help you overcome a worldly obstacle or fulfil your worldly desires. So the god of wealth can help you become wealthy if you approach him in the right way. The god of love can shower his blessings and help you find your right partner if you approach him the right way. The god of health can cure ailments which no doctor in the world can if you approach him the right way.

There are many people who wonder how the gods of heaven fulfils the wishes of evil people. The fact is that the gods of heaven don't weigh the past evil acts of the person while bestowing his grace on the person. The god of wealth or any other gods will grant you your wish if you approach them the right way. The evil acts of a person are taken care of by the higher law of karma. The responsibility of the gods of heaven are limited to the roles they're allotted just as the responsibility of the minister of a state is limited to the role one is allotted. The minister will grant you your wish if you approach him the right way and so do the gods.

What is the right way? The right way is described in the Vedas , the oldest Hindu scripture. Says Krishna to Arjuna : "All livings beings are born of food. Food is produced from rain. Rain is due to sacrifice."

The birth of a child happens when a man and woman make love. The union of semen and foetus produces the baby child. The fetus is nurtured through blood which in turn depends on food. Food crops thrive on rain. Though modern technology might not depend on rain and have other means to produce food the fact remains that rain balances the eco-system and influences the workings of our body in many ways. Rain and every aspect of nature is controlled by the gods of heaven. There is a sun god, a rain god, fire god, water god, and so on. Human beings on earth can communicate with gods through sacrifices. These sacrifices are explained in detail in the Vedas.

Most people on earth laugh when Hindus worship idols. They don't understand that all that the Hindu is trying to do is worship the gods of heaven relating to his or her problem. **Human beings have millions of problems and so Hindus have millions of gods to take care of them**. Imagine a vast country like India. There's a president, a prime minister, a chief minister for every state. Then there are other ministers looking after different departments. Under these ministers thousands of other government officials are appointed. Now if you want to get your work done through a government official wouldn't you go out of your way to please him or her? Wouldn't you approach him or her and say words which please the government official? We all do it every single day and justify that it's part of our life. So what's wrong in worshipping an idol which represents a god of heaven? You don't see the god of heaven in the idol and you think the Hindu is worshipping a stone. You don't understand the law of the lunar sphere and so you're wrong.

The worship of thousands of gods by the Hindus is justified but what the Hindu doesn't understand is this: **that the gods of heaven can help you overcome any obstacle of the world and can fulfil your worldly desire but they can't help you become perfect**. Perfection is a different game altogether and we will cover that as we move forward.

In this context, Krishna points out that the worshippers of gods proceed to the lunar sphere and have to return back to earth as they haven't perfected the yoga of transcendence.

Next comes those human beings who are attached to their ancestors. These beings reach the world of ancestors. The world of ancestors is a part of the lunar sphere. When you die you can meet up with your father, mother or anyone else in your family who has passed away. In fact, there are many psychics on earth who can help you connect with your ancestors in the lunar sphere. This is very much possible. There are a good number of sharp and highly integrated beings in existence on earth at any point of time who can help you connect with your ancestors in the lunar sphere.

The worshippers of elementals proceed to elementals. We all know in this earth life there are crooks whose only objective is to take advantage of other people. When they die they proceed to the elemental world. This world is between the earth world and the lunar sphere, says Krishna. They too return back to earth after a brief period of rest.

"Full of vile and wicked conduct I fling these deluded souls into demoniac wombs." Krishna is firm in his denunciation of those who are wicked.

Demoniac wombs could be the wombs of tigers, snakes, reptiles or even human beings with crooked and wicked characters. So those who live in the senses and think day and night that there is no great pleasure existing in this universe other than the body and the mind get hurled into these demoniac wombs after a brief period of rest.

It's important to note that Krishna hasn't revealed any minimum number of years that the souls spend in the lunar sphere before they return back to earth. We saw earlier that one year in the lunar sphere is equal to 360 years in the earth world. So if one spends even one year in the lunar sphere by the time one returns back to earth 360 years would have already passed on earth.

There are two authentic and accepted manuscripts which talk about life after death. They are *Garud Puran* and *Kapilaopadesh.*

Kapilopadesh was written by the sage Kapila many years before *Bhagavad Gita* became popular among the masses. Says Krishna to Arjuna: "Of the sages I am the perfected sage , Kapila."

Kapila has written: "The way to Yama's abode is ninety-nine thousand yogjanas but it is covered in three muhurtas (roughly around two and a half hours on earth).

Yama was the first man to die and he became the god of death. Yogjanas is nothing but a unit of measurement just like miles to measure astral travel.

One yojana is approximately eight miles. So according to Kapila it takes around two and a half hours for the departed soul to reach the kingdom of death which is close to the lunar sphere.

However , *Garud Puran* , the second most revered text , differs from Kapila. *Garud Puran* was written by wise sages many years after *Bhagavad Gita* became popular. It says: "Eight six thousand yojanas it takes for the departed soul to reach the kingdom of death. The departed soul travels two hundred and forty-seven yojanas every day."

So if we divide 86000 yojanas by 247 it comes to around 348 earth days. So a minimum of 348 days is spent in just travelling to the kingdom of death which is close to the lunar sphere.

The time taken to reach the lunar sphere and the years which one spends in the lunar sphere before one returns back to earth remains a mystery.

"He who sees the multiplicity of beings as abiding in the self and plurality of beings as proceeding from the self attains to me," Krishna says. "My devotees come to me directly. They do not reach the lunar sphere and return back. They come to my abode."

Electric Sphere

"Fire, light, day, bright fortnight, six months of the sun's northern course passing in time marked by these the knower's of supreme attain to me and never return back ,Krishna affirms."

The electric sphere is the world beyond the earth and the lunar sphere. The electric sphere governs and surrounds the world of heaven. Imagine the electric sphere to be a much higher vibration of your mind where you can go beyond the earth and heaven into the world of cosmic creation, maintenance ,and destruction. In the electric world exists three entities. The god of creation, the god of maintenance , and the god of destruction. The god of creation is called Brahma. The god of maintenance is called Vishnu, and the god of destruction is called Shiva.

We saw earlier that in the earth world force is physical and matter is sensible. In the lunar sphere force is psychic and matter is fine particles. However , in the electric sphere the vibration is so high that it's no longer possible to differentiate matter and force. You can hardly tell whether electricity is force or matter.

Fire, light, day, bright fortnight, and six months of the sun's southern course are the favourable agents of death which transport those free souls (ones who have transcended the three constituents) beyond the lunar sphere into the electric sphere.

"Confining the mind to the heart, fixing the life force in the crown, intent on yoga one merges with me and never returns back into this world," **declares Krishna.**

There are only two things you need to be aware of to transcend the three constituents, Krishna asserts.

First , you need to learn to fix the mind in the heart. What does that mean? There are only two places where the mind is stable and calm. They are the center of your heart and the center of your eye-brows. In all other places the mind will wander , says Krishna. When the mind is trained to be seated at the center of the heart, your mind won't wander and associate itself with the agents of change. The supreme self within will shine in true splendour and help you to be in constant communication with itself. So simply close your eyes for five minutes every day and imagine your mind seated in the heart. Keep it simple and with training and persistence you will perfect it.

Second , once you've trained your mind to be confined in the heart you have to then learn to fix the life force in the center of the crown (the center of your eyes is called the crown). What does that mean? Life force is called "prana" - that which facilitates awareness in you through breathing. Prana isn't breathing but that agent which causes breathing. This breathing first acts upon the lungs, the lungs upon the heart , the heart upon the blood circulation which in turn acts on the brain. The brain then acts on the mind which produces awareness of the outside world. So prana is a very subtle thing – it's the agent which causes awareness. Once you're able to confine the mind to the heart you'll notice the movements of prana. In time you'll be able to center it between your eye brows.

How does one consistently train the mind to be confined in the heart and the life force in the crown? Is it complicated? Does it require you to spend 10 hours in meditation? No , says Krishna.. "To the single minded yogin in perpetual communion with me I am always easily accessible," Krishna tells Arjuna.

Confining the mind to the heart and the life force in the crown is an effect, the cause of which is yoga - the intention to transcend - the intention to merge with the divine, the intention to disassociate oneself with the agents of change. Simply focus on these intentions and these will drive you to take the right action to get the desired results. Every single person will effortlessly reach the goal one day , predicts Krishna. Simply begin your journey today and if you've already started on this journey firm it up a little bit.

So these free souls, the ones who have transcended the three constituents reach the electric sphere and here they meet another perfected soul which transports them to a world beyond the electric sphere, where the soul lives eternally no more to be born or to die.

Says Krishna to Arjuna : "All worlds' up to and including Brahma are won and lost but on reaching me you don't return back. I alone am Time imperishable wrecking the dissolution of beings."

Time doesn't spare even the god of creation, the god of maintenance and the god of destruction. Brahma , Vishnu and Shiva all have to die. All of them have to perish when the cosmic dissolution happens. We'll cover the cosmic dissolution in a later chapter but for the moment it suffices to understand **that all of the three worlds' earth sphere, lunar sphere and electric sphere are finite in time**. All these three worlds succumb to the destruction of time. Brahma , Vishnu and Shiva are all perfected souls having transcended the three constituents. However, since they're placed with the responsibility of creation, maintenance and dissolution they appear to be finite in time and get annihilated when the cosmic dissolution happens.

Important note to the ardent devotees of Brahma , Vishnu , and Shiva:

The death of Brahma ,Vishnu, and Shiva at the end of cosmic dissolution has to be viewed as the end of the creator, sustainer and destroyer of the universe and not as the death of Brahma , Vishnu , and Shiva per se as all these three gods are perfected souls having

manifested from the navel, heart and forehead of Krishna respectively. Since the universe itself no longer exists these perfected souls no longer need to exist and must be annihilated.
The free soul however has a choice to live eternally in another world beyond the electric sphere.

Brahma lok

Those free souls who chose to merge with the supreme travel beyond the electric sphere and are escorted into the world of Brahma lok by the favourable agents of death. "Lok" means world or sphere.

These free souls, enjoys wide powers and have the jurisdiction to use it for the good of many. The only power they don't possess is creation and destruction of the whole universe.

"All powers except the creative comes to the jiva (perfected soul) and if it likes to have bodies and work in different parts of the world, it can do so," says Swami Vivekananda. " If it orders all the gods of heaven to come before it, if it wants its forefathers to come, they all appear at its command. Such are its powers that it never feels any more pain, and if it wants, it can live in Brahmaloka through all eternity. The only deathless place is Brahmaloka, where alone there is no birth and death."

The Brahma lok shouldn't be confused with Brahma , the god of creation. This world is superior to the electric sphere. The earth sphere, the lunar sphere and the electric sphere are all finite in time and have to eventually succumb to the destruction of time. **However , Brahma lok is the only world which doesn't perish even when the three worlds end.**

"Beyond the three worlds is another eternal unmanifest world , O Arjuna," Krishna explains. "It perishes not even when all beings perish"

In the Brahma lok there is neither force nor matter , but both are merged in the primal energy. In this world the individual soul (jiva) contemplates the whole universe as one- the sum total of all energy. The jiva or individual soul experiences for the first time the intensity of Purusha (universal soul). However, this world is still not the absolute for there is still multiplicity for the jiva. The jiva has not yet united with the Purusha.

"Even the gods and the great seers do not know my origin for in all respects I am the origin of gods and the seers," Krishna tells Arjuna.

Even Brahma and Shiva , the gods of creation and destruction ,and all the free souls , don't know the supreme self completely, Krishna says, pointing out that he was the one who brought them into existence.

It's very interesting to note that a human being sitting in one corner of the earth can communicate with the solar systems, and go beyond them into the world of lunar sphere. Humans can also communicate with the gods, such as Brahma, the god of creation and Shiva, the god of destruction. All this is possible if you step up the vibration of your mind, says Krishna.

Consider the world of Purusha (the world beyond Brahma Lok, and how the Jiva unites with the Purusha.

"There the sun shines not nor the moon much less the earthly fire," Krishna says. "That is my abode reaching which none returns back."

The four parallel worlds up to Brahma lok can be perceived and expressed but Purusha the world beyond the Brahma lok can't be expressed or perceived. Why is that so? **All perception and expression are possible only until such time that there is duality.** The perfected soul on reaching Brahma lok perceives and experiences the entire earth world, the lunar sphere and the electric world as being merged in the primal energy. However, there is still multiplicity for the perfected soul as it has not united with the Purusha. Once it unites with the Purusha it loses its identification. No more can it return back. No more does it have the ability to perceive and express for it has become one with the supreme.

There is only one ruler of the universe and that is God. No one can become God. Says Krishna: "I am the lord of all the four worlds- (the earth world, the lunar sphere, the electric sphere and Brahma lok). He who knows me to be without a beginning and without an end knows me completely and will attain to me. O Arjuna."

So the free souls have a choice to stay in Brahma lok eternally or merge with the supreme and never return back. Why don't they return back? Because there's no need. The game is over, the end achieved.

" **Deprived of knowledge as a result of cravings, man tends to worship other deities and tends to follow other disciplines being constrained by their inborn nature," Krishna warns.**

"After many repeated births the individual soul attains perfection knowing Krishna is all. Such souls , O Arjuna ,are very rare"

Understand Krishna's meaning is that the three agents of change make you think and act in a particular manner , binding you to the law of karma. Krishna says we act ignorantly because we don't know the laws of the spiritual world. This ignorance on our part makes us believe and disbelieve certain facts and theories about life after death. However, Krishna maintains that if you apply yourself to the yoga of transcendence and train yourself to step up the vibration of your mind all the laws of the spiritual world would be revealed to you in total.

The four parallel worlds are revealed to all those blessed souls who sincerely apply themselves to the yoga of transcendence and work diligently towards stepping up the vibration of the mind.

When your mind is at a lower vibration you only perceive the earth world; when you step it up further you go beyond the earth world into the lunar sphere and communicate with the gods of heaven. If you firm it up a little more you gain access to the world of electric sphere , and if you desire to move even farther up you end up in Brahma lok. All these four worlds can be perceived in succession by the individual soul. These four worlds exist in parallel and can be accessed by any individual who applies themselves to yoga , says Krishna. **What the wise beings call 'ignorance' is nothing but the lack of knowledge of these four worlds.** Knowledge of these four worlds help a human being to refine one's actions , leading one to the world of perfection.- the world of Brahma lok.

Buddha, Christ, Mohammed, Guru Nanak, Ramakrishna, Ramana Maharishi, Vivekananda, Yogananda and many other great souls were completely aware of these four parallel worlds. They might have chosen not to talk about it or express it to their followers ,but if you observe all their actions and their personality you'll discover that they were never too much concerned about the cravings of the body and the desires of the mind. The word spirit or spiritual scattered across various scriptures and sacred texts is nothing but the qualities or characteristics which enables one to reach the Brahma lok- the world of perfection. God has better things to do than revealing the existence of different worlds again and again. Krishna has revealed it once and there it ends. The great souls who followed him simply lived that wonderful life full of divine characteristics and pristine qualities and became a role model for centuries to come.

"He who believes not believes not even after seeing." says Krishna to Arjuna. It's interesting to note that Krishna and every other wise being in the world didn't spend time in text torturing explaining every single aspect of the scriptures with reasoning. They were aware of the flaws of human nature arising from of the three agents of change operating in every individual. So they simply spoke and the world listened.

"The potent jiva when it gains a fresh body carries with it all the past impressions and intentions just as the air when it travels carries the scent of its abode," Krishna says.

You have to simply get this one thing right. You are complete. You are all powerful. You can never be destroyed. That which isn't complete that which isn't powerful and can be destroyed is not you -. It's the agent of change. These agents of change force you to seek new bodies to work out your desired experiences. **Train yourself to step up the vibration of your mind and dissociate yourself from these agents of change and you'll no longer feel the need for acquiring new bodies.**

"There was never a time when you and I never

existed," Krishna explains." You know them not . I know them all. "

Krishna doesn't grieve for the living and for those who have died. He says you've taken human birth countless times before and will continue to do so in the future until you've learned to transcend the three constituents.

"There is nothing to grieve ," Krishna advises. You have married millions of time before; you have had million of fathers, mothers, brothers and sisters, sons and daughters before. You have died millions of time before. What is there to grieve about?

****

Although we've seen that it isn't necessary that there shall be the memory of past lives. Yet at the same time, we're in a position to assert that there are instances which show that this memory does come, and that each one of us will get back this memory in that life in which he will become free. Then alone you'll find that this world is a dream; then alone you'll realize in your soul that we're but actors and the world is a stage. Then alone will this idea of non-attachment come to you like thunder.

Thirst for enjoyment, clinging on to life and this world, will vanish for ever . The mind will see clearly as daylight how many times all these factors existed for you, how many millions of time you had fathers and mothers, sons and daughters , husbands and wives, relatives and friends, wealth and power. They came and went. How many times you were on the topmost crest of the wave, and how many times you were down at the bottom of despair. When memory will bring all these to you, then alone will you stand as a hero and smile when the world frowns upon you. Then alone will you stand up and say "I care not for thee even, O Death. What terrors hast thou for me?' This will come to all.

Swami Vivekananda

****

Re-birth or re-incarnation is a law, not a belief.

It doesn't matter whether you believe in it or not , it exists. Human beings want to perceive it through the senses and intellect , just as one touches the wall or eats food or sees data in one computer being transferred to another. Through the senses and the intellect one can't perceive these higher truths. It's only through increasing the vibration of your mind that these subtle truths could be perceived and comprehended.

"The deluded do not see him moving out, staying in and associating in connection with the three constituents , Krishna explains. "The wise knows it all."

When the body falls, the soul moves out of the body along with the subtle impressions and intentions and travels to the lunar sphere. Subsequently it returns back to earth into another new body. The deluded don't see these fine movements. The wise knows it all, says Krishna.

When we're alive we fail to notice the subtle movements of the agents of change operating within our body. It's these agents of change which makes us think and act in a particular manner. That which is called characteristics or personality of a person is influenced by these agents of change.

"You might be a very hot tempered person by

nature till today but from this moment you can change your nature to a level headed and calm person if you identify the agent of anger and understand that you are not the agent of anger," Krishna says. " Anger will no longer rule over you. " This is very much possible , Krishna affirms.

You can think about a million reasons which make you angry and try a ton of tactics to stay away from these damaging thoughts, but the agent of anger which is pre-dominant in you will have its way and burst out. However, if you learn to identify the agent of anger and manage to transcend it, it will disappear instantly.

To defeat any problem that you face, and any obstacle that you want to overcome, spend some time identifying the agent of change operating within you and train yourself to disassociate with that agent by increasing the vibration of your mind.

"Him the weapons cannot cut, the water cannot wet, the air cannot dry, and fire cannot burn. So , O Arjuna, grieve not for the dead. These two paths which I revealed to you- one through which the soul travels to the lunar sphere and returns back to earth and the other through which the soul merges with me and never returns back are eternal. So grieve not for the dead and apply yourself to the yoga of transcendence always."

Arjuna raises a important question to Krishna here. "O Krishna, those who have led a life of righteousness filled with complete faith in you but have failed to perfect the yoga of transcendence in this life ,what happens to them? Do all their good acts disappear like the scattered clouds of summer?"

In response, Krishna says: "The doer of good never comes to grief , O Arjuna. Neither in this world nor in the world to come. Having spent time in the meritorious world of lunar sphere and after a long sojourn there he returns back to be born in the house of pure and prosperous householders or in some rare cases in the house of wise yogins."

It's important to understand that the impressions of good deeds are never lost. They are retained just as the impression of ignorant deeds. Krishna doesn't believe in sin. He believes only in error arising due to ignorance of the spiritual laws. Krishna says the soul which hasn't perfected the art of transcendence reaches the lunar sphere , spends good time there , and then is reborn again in the house of prosperous and pure householders. In a few lucky cases the soul is born in the house of wise yogins. The wise yogin is one who has mastered the yoga of transcendence. This wise yogin might be poor or rich but it doesn't matter. The wise yogin respects and practises the yoga of transcendence which facilitates the right environment for the newly born soul.

Continuing, Krishna says: "There he acquires the memory of the ideas of his previous bodies and labours hard to achieve perfection. Even though he is not a master, he is attracted by his prior discipline and moves forward. Thus moving forward with total dedication he attains perfection through repeated births and merges with the supreme."

The yogic impressions of the earlier lifetime's surfaces in the individual when other ordinary and past impressions have given way. "None of your efforts in the path of yoga go waste," says Krishna. "Every thought, every action and every movement in that direction, is retained and will surface in your mind at the right moment helping you remember the heroic attempts made towards yoga in your earlier lifetimes. The way to the supreme is the way forward and not the way behind.

Not a step back says Krishna.. Move forward and apply yourself towards yoga, Krishna stresses.

"The yogin is superior to the performers of austerities, superior to even the knower of Vedas, and those who excel in works. So grieve not for the dead , O Arjuna , and at all times engage in yoga. Him I deem the most integrated who worships me with absolute faith, his inner self completely absorbed in yoga."

The one who has mastered the yoga of transcendence is his favourite, Krishna reveals. "Such a person is superior to all beings on earth, superior even than the person of perfect knowledge of God, superior to even the person of flawless action and results. That integrated soul rules over the three worlds, so O Arjuna ,always engage yourself in yoga of transcendence."

"Neither by the Vedas, nor through severe penance or sacrifices, neither by giving of gifts can I be attained , O Arjuna,"
"To the single minded Yogin in perpetual communion with me I am always easily accessible."

"Devoid of delusion, overcoming the flaws of attachment, firm in spirituality, free of lust, released from the dualities of pain and pleasure one can reach me. For such is my nature."

These last three quotes of Krishna form the whole essence of the *Bhagavad Gita*. Krishna says you may not be able to reach him by sitting cross-legged in the Himalayas and meditating for long years. You may not reach him by performing all those Vedic sacrifices intended to please the gods in heaven. You may not reach him by giving gifts of charity.

There are four characteristics which you have to watch out for to reach Krishna:

1) You have to learn to overcome the **flaws of attachment**. We'll cover

this in great detail in a separate chapter. Krishna says that there's nothing wrong in forming relationships and associations but one has to remember that every relationship carries with it the flaw of attachment. The flaw of attachment means an agent which binds one being to another- a father to a son, a mother to her child a husband to his wife. This agent operates within you and makes you think and act in a particular manner , binding you within the confines of the earth world and the lunar sphere. This agent , says Krishna , has to be observed and conquered for one to move beyond the lunar sphere.

2) You have to **master the spiritual laws** , remember the four parallel worlds , and strive to conduct your daily activities in line with these laws to transcend to the world beyond the lunar sphere.

3) You have to be free of lust- We'll cover this in a separate chapter.

Krishna doesn't view lust as a sin . He terms it ignorance arising out of low vibration of your mind. Krishna simply says not to worry if you've lusted a million times before. It doesn't matter. Simply increase the vibration of your mind and the agent of lust will disappear.

4) You have to train **your mind to be fixed in the heart** or in the center of your eye-brows at all

times. When you succeed your mind won't wander and it will remain in perpetual communion with Krishna.

These four characteristics form the yoga of transcendence and will help you reach Krishna.

What Krishna wants to convey is this: Giving charity, meditating cross-legged, performing sacrifices and such related activities , will help you purify your mind and makes you fit for the yoga of transcendence; but these actions by themselves aren't necessary to reach him. He who has developed and strived towards achieving perfection in those four characteristics can only reach Krishna . Others can't.

Meditation, sacrifice, charity and other related activities only inspire us in the path of yoga but they're not yoga by themselves. It's good to meditate and give to charity but these actions don't help you reach the world of perfection. They only inspire you to move forward. The world of perfection can be attained only when one acquires those four characteristics.

In the earth world you'll come across many powerful beings who can look at your face and predict your past and your future in seconds. There are those who can heal you by touch, who can create anything out of thin air, who can become invisible at will, who can predict the exact time of your death, and walk on water. All these seem supernatural to human beings and many rush to worship these entities as gods and to seek advice from them. But on close observation you'll discover that most of these supernatural beings don't practise the yoga of transcendence and don't possess the four characteristics described earlier. These supernatural beings , through many lifetimes of practice , have simply mastered certain skills not common among men and women. However , take any great soul and if you observe carefully you'll find one common thing in them. They all would have achieved mastery of those four key characteristics.

It might be true that some great souls would have healed people by touch and performed other few supernatural activities. But those supernatural activities didn't form their agenda for life and weren't the reasons why the world remembers them many years after their passing away from earth.

Krishna doesn't require you to fly in air or walk in water. He doesn't require that you should be able to read a person's mind and predict the time of his death. He doesn't force you to sit in meditation for long hours or give money to charity. In fact, he doesn't care even if you don't heal a single person through touch. He simply wants you to strive towards the yoga of transcendence with love and faith, with a smile and a deep knowing. It's easy to inspire people around you if you're inspired. Krishna wants you to be inspired.

How to easily communicate with perfected souls in Brahma lok.

Take a notepad and on the first page write these three points:

1) It's easy to communicate with perfected souls.

2) I'm going to communicate constantly with Buddha from today. In this example we use Buddha but you can replace Buddha with the perfected soul of your choice. It could be Christ, Mohammed, Ramakrishna, Vivekananda, Ramana Maharishi, Guru Nanak, Moses , or any other wise being.

3) I'm going to keep a daily record of my experiences through this wonderful communication.

Now put the notepad aside. Sit on the floor cross-legged , spine erect , and simply close your eyes. Breathe slowly. Say to yourself:"It's easy to communicate with Buddha."

Now imagine the earth world with all its elements (7 billion human beings, plants, animals, mountains, oceans and every other moving and non-moving object) rushing to unite with your consciousness in the center of your heart. Imagine this scene vividly. Welcome all these elements into the center of your heart Reject none. Allow them to reside in your heart and to become one with your consciousness. Let the entire earth world cease to exist. Let only the consciousness of the earth world exist. Carry forward that giant wave of earth consciousness existing in your heart into the lunar sphere.

In the lunar sphere meet Kandarapa , the god of love and touch his feet. Meet Kuber , the god of wealth , and prostrate yourself before him. Meet Danwantri , the god of health , and convey your respect to him. Spend time with your ancestors if you wish. Chat with them and thank them for everything that they've done for you. Move around the lunar sphere and get an idea of the pleasure and activities happening within. Watch how even the gods fight, how they chase women , and how even the gods die. Discriminate and remind your consciousness that heaven is a beautiful place but it isn't your final destination. Saying goodbye to all the gods , move forward into the electric sphere.

Dance with Shiva in the electric sphere. Meet Saraswati , the goddess of learning who is Brahma's consort. Seek her blessings. Touch Vishnu's feet and feel blessed. Meet Lakshmi, the goddess of prosperity who is Vishnu's consort. Thank her for treating you well and taking care of you in the earth world. Spend some time meditating with Shiva. Notice the high vibration of energy in the electric sphere. Discover how force and matter has become one in the electric sphere. Request Shiva to introduce you to his consort, the goddess Kali, the destroyer of evil in the world. Seek her blessing which will serve you a life time. Meet Ganesha ,the son of Shiva and the destroyer of obstacles. Prepare modak (a special Indian sweet) and offer it to Ganesha.

Spend some time with all the three gods and their consorts and share with them your concerns about the earth world and what they feel could be done to make the earth world a much healthier and loving place. Ask them for specific suggestions which you as an individual can implement. Talk to them and they will help you in ways you can never imagine. Bidding them goodbye and seeking their blessings , now move forward into the world of Brahma lok.

Greet all the perfected souls here. Meet Buddha, Mohammed, Jesus, Moses, Guru Nanak, Ramakrishna, Vivekananda and the head of every other religion. Prostrate yourself before them and spend some time with each of them. Ask Buddha to reveal the secret of renunciation. What should one give up this very moment? Meet Mohammed and ask him why Muslims are ready to give up their life for his sake? Ask him to reveal the secret of brotherhood. Meet Ramakrishna, - the man who embraced the three religions of Hindism, Islam , and Christianity in one life. Ask him to disclose the secret of his devotion and to share one quality which every Hindu could implement in their daily worship of gods. Meet Vivekananda and request him to share the secret of his perfect knowledge.

Meet Jesus and touch his holy feet. Request him to reveal the secret of his pure love. Ask him when he would be visiting earth the next time. Meditate for some time in this holy place where all perfected souls reside. Celebrate your entry into the Brahma lok. Meet the perfected soul you had planned to visit in Brahma lok. Spend quality time with him or her. Ask questions, have fun, and open your heart . Be attentive to the answers, and respect the silence of the perfected soul. Seek their blessings, and don't be shy to ask for help. Ask for guidance and above all a chance to visit and communicate with them again.

Open your eyes and you're back to the earth world.

How to effortlessly increase the vibration of your mind.

Take your notepad, open a new page , and write these five points.

1) I'm as good as my vibration of mind. The higher the vibration , the finer will be my awareness, with a lower vibration means a more confused awareness.

2) I'm convinced that all confusion, doubt and differences arises due to low vibration of mind; and all clarity, abundance, love, peace and compassion arises out of a higher vibration of mind. I will strive to remember this law during my daily life.

3) That area in my life which has a low vibration suffers. If my vibration relating to abundance is low then that area suffers. If my vibration relating to relationship is poor then that area suffers. If my vibration relating to health is bad then that area suffers. I will pick one area of my life where the vibration is very low and set it right.

4) The secret of increasing the rate of vibration is to identify and relate to an object in nature with a higher level of vibration. This object could be a wise soul, a strong animal, a mountain, a flower or any other divine aspect of nature. If scarcity is tormenting me, I will fix my mind on the gigantic ocean and feel its abundance. I will watch how river water is continuously pouring into the ocean and getting discharged the next moment. I

will observe how the ocean creates a series of waves in one sequence and destroys it the next moment. I will meditate on the heart of the ocean which is always full and stable and in peace with itself. **The ocean never runs after water. It owns the water and it's always full no matter how much it gives.** I will train my mind to focus on the serenity of the ocean and to inherit its abundant qualities.

5) If I suffer from health issues I will concentrate on the strength of an elephant or the image of a strong god. If I feel the urge for elegance I will enter into the consciousness of the lion. If I crave for a more cheerful nature I will fix my mind on the splendor of the rose or the sunflower. If I'm having trouble with purity I'll attempt to merge into the consciousness of Buddha or Christ. I have endless choices. I'll remember that I'm not trying to become anything. I'm simply taking the help of nature to correct that part of my personality which is at a lower rate of vibration.

Now put the notepad aside. Arrange your daily schedule to get up every morning before others in your house and take your position on the floor. Sit cross-legged and enjoy the morning silence. Take pleasure in the warmth of your being. Don't seek anything. Everything is going to be yours very soon.

Read the five points you've written in the notepad aloud. Now close your eyes and imagine your mind seated firmly in the center of your heart. If your mind wanders take the help of your finger and place it at the center of your heart and you'll notice that your mind will follow your finger to the heart. Enjoy the whole process but don't make it tough on you. This isn't an examination and there's nothing to fail. You simply have to get it right.

Now comes the interesting part. After you fix your mind in the center of your heart and allow it to remain in that position for five minutes.

Then imagine that your mind, followed by your consciousness, is leaving you through the center of the heart. Just close your eyes and imagine that your consciousness is leaving you through that center and moving towards that object of nature which you've identified earlier. In this example let's take the ocean. So basically you're allowing your consciousness to enter into the consciousness of the ocean. When I mean entering I literally mean entering. Imagine that your consciousness has now entered into the ocean. Feel the personality of the gigantic ocean. Dance with the waves. Watch as the ocean is always full and stable. Water is continuously pouring in and getting discharged. The ocean is always abundant. Enjoy the whole experience.

As you enjoy your union with the ocean take care not to let your consciousness jump back into your body. Let your consciousness stay there in the ocean. This is very important. Allow your consciousness to reside inside the ocean; don't be in a hurry to bring it back into your being. Let it drink the abundance of the ocean. The mistake which many make is that they hurry to analyse what they experience and they pull their consciousness into their body.

Don't do that. You own your consciousness. It is yours. It will come back. Allow it to come back with power and abundance. Allow your consciousness to rest in the heart of the ocean for a short duration. You don't have to do it for a long time. The intensity is important.

Enjoy the whole experience and when you are filled , jump back in.

Do this every day for fifteen minutes- The first five minutes fix your mind on the center of your heart, and during the remaining 10 minutes allow your consciousness to enter into the object chosen, be it a rose or a lion or anything else. Just enter into it. Feel the vibration. When done jump back into your body. You'll notice a remarkable change in your vibration in a very short time.

"He wins peace, O Arjuna, in whom mind enters objects of desire as river water enters into a full and stable ocean waiting to be filled, and not in one seeking desires."

Abundance is all about owning that which never depletes. Dry lakes are never abundant. It's only the ocean which is always abundant. It owns the water. Water pours in and water gets discharged but the ocean is always full and stable. You own the earth and the heaven. Never forget that!

Chapter 4

How I overcame the flaws of attachment and mastered the yoga of detachment and how you too can also.

"What which men call renunciation, O Arjuna , know that to be yoga. He who is not attached to the senses and to his works, who has discarded all mental constructions scales to the peak of yoga. Know him to be a yogin."

"Mental constructions" is the watch word. The other word for mental constructions is individuality. Krishna says that aspect of your individuality which remains after you've discarded all mental constructions is worthy to be known.

I want to reveal to you the fantastic side of your personality. This aspect of your personality isn't about what you're good at. It has nothing to do with your characteristics and passions. I'm talking of a different kind of individuality- that which is fun to work with, easy to access , and above all that which makes you feel complete no matter how you fare in your life. I want you to pay close attention as this aspect of your personality can significantly enhance your forward journey.

A little about me. I am 39 years old and until the age of 30 I used to take all my thoughts very seriously. If I get a pleasure thought it will be followed by an act of pleasure. If I get a painful thought it will be followed by a painful experience. This was how I lived. Thought to me was the cause and experience the effect.

I had only to get up in the morning and these thoughts would start trickling in one after another and I would relate to all of them and go through those cycle of experiences of pleasure and pain. Looking back I sometime wonder who lived those 30 years. Me or my thoughts? Me or my experiences?

Now during this time I used to work with a fortune 500 company in India and had to travel by train on weekends for business . In one of my train trips I picked up a book, *Talks with Swami Vivekananda* , and I started reading a few pages. It was interesting. I had no real fascination for spirituality until that time. I only knew that a higher power called God existed and I never doubted it ; but I was never too keen to explore it either. As I read through the pages of the book one conversation between Vivekananda and his disciple struck my attention. Vivekananda narrated a verse from *Bhagavad Gita* where Krishna tells to Arjuna :

"Futile are your desires. Futile are your actions. Futile are your experiences if you do not know your real nature."

And I thought , what is Krishna talking about? In one single sentence he had knocked everything out of me. My desires, my actions , and my experiences..I was curious what this "real nature" was all about.

Then Vivekananda went on to explain about soul, god , and everything in spirituality in a beautiful manner that was music to my ears. I had never felt so much peace and power. So that's how I got started in this spiritual journey and in the last five years have been blessed to write nine bestselling books which have been accepted very well. I've been fortunate to be in a position to share the spiritual messages full time but I have to admit that from the day knowledge knocked on my doors life was horrible for me. I discovered that I had such an ordinary personality. Whenever I tried to put the knowledge to use my past thoughts and past actions would intervene and justify its stupidity. And the end result was I wasn't going anywhere. It was so frustrating. had access to the best knowledge . I had the will to implement it but my own past actions, thoughts, and personality would banish these beautiful words of wisdom. Life was hell and most people thought I had gone mad as my spirit wanted to go in one direction and my mind in another . And my body as usual wouldn't listen to anything and anyone.

Now there was one good thing which happened during this moment of personal crisis. I never missed my moment of silence in the morning and evening. Every day I used to spend the morning and evening time in prayers and silence. I don't know how I formed that habit but that came naturally to me. I never missed a single day. Everything else was secondary. I started the day respecting the source and ended the day with a thank you to the source. No matter what happened during the day I would never miss my morning and evening time of silence and I think it's this simple habit of silence and prayers which brought about the giant change and discovery which I'm going to reveal to you . This is a change which will provide you with a very powerful tool to master the yoga of transcendence.

Secret No 1

Happiness is always associated with struggle. That happiness which isn't associated with struggle is called pleasure and it's of very little use to human beings. Growth is and will be associated with struggle.

Struggle is inevitable. **If you're not struggling it means you're not growing**. Now I want to make sure you understand what struggle is. I'm not talking about the struggle to pay your bills and fulfil the desires of your mind which keep changing every single moment. That struggle is futile.

Says Krishna to Arjuna; "Give up the struggle with the causes of your current circumstance and give up the struggle with the future effects of these underlying causes."

Struggling with past events and past associations are the causes of your current circumstances. Never struggle with that. It's in vain. Give it up this moment , says Krishna. Procrastination, anger, impatience, negative attitude, lack of foresight, inability to form good relationships – all these aren't the causes for personal failure ; rather they are the effects of low vibration of your mind.

Fear of failure, insecurity over paying bills, self doubt in attaining your goals and like thoughts and concerns are the future effects of your current personality. Never struggle with that. Give it up this moment, advises Krishna.

Struggle with just one thing : Your current personality versus the knowledge you have. That struggle is the best and the grandest, "the struggle of your current personality v/s the knowledge you have" When you struggle in that direction you'll eventually achieve everything you set your mind to.

The gap isn't between thoughts and action. The real gap is between knowledge and personality and it's this gap which influences ordinary thoughts, slows down action and makes you feel redundant or of less value.

The first step then is to know more. By knowing more I mean know more about yourself. Your thoughts , your mind and your source. It's very important you do that. The easiest way to get started is to train yourself to increase the vibration of your mind.

The second step is to work with your personality. What happens when you read an insightful book or watch a transformational video. You suddenly feel inspired and feel "Yes ,I too can do it." Now observe carefully the workings of your mind. You gained access to knowledge which made you feel confident that you too can achieve your goals. However , you notice something interesting as you move forward. No sooner do you attempt to put the knowledge into practice something intrudes and blocks your way. Your own current personality acts as an obstacle in putting these great ideas forward.

Secret No 2:

We all have a split personality. Know and acknowledge that split personality.

Every human being has two personalities. One that is subject to change and the other that is changeless. The one that is subject to change is a "mock up" personality while the other that is changeless is the divine aspect of our being. Let's first talk about the personality that's subject to change and how we can allow it to get the results that we want.

Whenever I was faced with a big problem I used to immediately start thinking about how to get out of the difficulty. The end result was I never resolved the problem because all I was doing was getting entangled more and more inside the involvement. I lacked two important things when faced with a problem:

1) Brilliant ideas which are more powerful than the weight of the current problem.

2) Free flowing energy to soak in these inspirational ideas and put them into practice.

I discovered very quickly that when my current circumstances were horrible my ideas were outright stupid and my energy sucked big time.

It was during these periods of turmoil that I discovered the fallacy of holding on to a frail personality, a personality which is subject to change based on events. How could all my enthusiasm, my inspiration my brilliant ideas my passion be crushed by a series of events? How could something external kill my personality?

We all work so hard on our personality and yet one event or a single mistake tears it apart. I couldn't buy this concept of a personality which wasn't able to resist the shocks and swings of life. Surely there must be an aspect stronger than what I had developed over the years.

Enter the Divine Personality

Krishna advises Arjuna: "That personality which is created as a result of your past experiences ,no matter how ugly or beautiful it may seem to be ,will one day be completely destroyed "

Give up your mock personality. Outgrow it, says Krishna.

How do we do that? Here is how I managed to do it.

During my moments of daily silence a thought came to me: Why would a bad experience ever chase me? What is the whole purpose of living through a horrible experience?

As these thoughts filled my mind a strange calmness descended into my being. Suddenly , a whole new pathway opened up for me. My old repetitive thoughts were nowhere to be seen. Now I wasn't in search for a thought. I was in search for a personality who could help me discover an answer.

A familiar voice from within spoke to me, not through thoughts and words but through gentle sounds which resonated with the core of my heart. This is what my divine personality revealed to me.

1) Don't panic. Everything isn't finished.

2) You have the power to create a new experience. Go ahead and create one.

3) Don't waste your entire energy trying to get out of your current problems. Simply acknowledge the current problem. That's all you have to do.

4) The easiest way to change your current

circumstances is to know the cycle of obstacles and allow it to destroy itself.

The Cycle of Obstacles And How It Can Shorten The Duration Of Your Problems

We can't drive away problems. We can only shorten the painful experience and when we manage to do that the problem disappears. A problem exists only as long as the need for a bad/troubling experience exists. When the painful experience has been acknowledged there will be no further need for the problem to exist. It has to go away. Here's how this phenomena happens.

We think. We act. We experience. Experience is an effect. However ,neither action nor thought is the real cause of the experience. The root causes of all experiences are impressions stored in the mind. It's these impressions which trigger thoughts which are then followed by actions and ultimately lead you to an experience. This is very interesting because **the length of a painful experience is directly proportional to the amount of troublesome painful impressions waiting to express itself in your mind**.

Cause	**Effect**

Deep Impressions

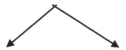

Painful & Pleasurable Experiences waiting to happen

Thought-Action-Experience

So what are impressions and how are they formed?

An impression is a reaction. Everything that we see, hear and touch is recorded in our mind in the form of subtle impressions. Consider an example. You go to work. You meet various people during the day. On your way back to home you see a pretty woman and you're greatly attracted. Before you go to sleep you recollect the events of the day and the only image which comes before your eyes is the vision of the beautiful woman. You can't help it. That image has formed a deep impression on your mind and forces you to keep thinking of it. You get up in the morning and that image still hasn't left you. You can't ignore these deep impressions and these impressions force you to think in a way unless you can counter it with a stronger impression.

The mind has an independent existence in the form of deep impressions.

Every deep impression in your mind is continuously seeking opportunities in this world to express itself and when it finds a suitable one it forces you to act in a particular way whether you want to or not . The end result is an event giving you that experience- pleasurable or painful.

You quickly discover that your current circumstance isn't the real problem. You also begin to understand that your thoughts and actions are caused by something more subtle- the deep impressions and it's these impressions which you have to observe and work with to bring about that much needed change.

Let's take a very practical example and turn it around. Assume you're in a horrible relationship and you're trying to get out of it or seek another partner. You try and try but nothing happens. Instead of fighting with the painful experience and trying to overcome it , simply ask yourself this question: **"How can I shorten this painful experience?"**

1) The first step would be to wisely acknowledge the painful experience. By acknowledging it I don't mean accepting it with grudge or a helpless attitude. Accept it with responsibility and knowledge. Say to yourself: It's impossible that I would personally choose a painful experience. However I do understand that an experience is an effect coming from a deep impression. The fact that I'm not able to discover the impression which caused this experience doesn't mean that the impression doesn't exist. It simply means I'm ignorant about the deep impression.

2) The second step is to go deep within yourself (and I will show you how to do that later through an exercise) and to find out the amount of related deep impressions existing in your mind waiting to express itself in the form of a painful experience.

This step is very important.

3) The third step is to understand the law of karma. It says: No deep impressions can be destroyed. **All impressions will have to be experienced by the seeker.** In the normal course of our daily life the law of karma takes all the deep impressions sitting inside our mind and seeks a suitable event or a person in the external world to unite these impressions to the experience. When it has found the right event/person it forces you to act in a particular way in relation to that person or event resulting in a painful or pleasurable experience. Pay close attention to this law of karma as it will enable you to break free from the cycle of obstacles.

The Knowledge of the Field and The Field Knower

"I know the field and I know myself as the field," Krisha tells Arjuna.

"Know me as the field knower also present in the field."

The deep impressions are the field and the experiencer is the field knower. The only objective of a deep impression is to seek a suitable experience. Once that's done the deep impression will no longer bother you. When one is ignorant of the field the law of karma takes over and it hunts for a person or event to help you achieve that experience.

The only purpose of any experience is to help you outgrow your personality, and to unite the field with the field knower. So instead of routing the impression through a person or event you become the agent to combine the field with the field knower.

You become the impression. You become the experience. When you do this you will no longer feel the necessity of prolonging the painful experience. **Your problem will disappear as soon as you unite the field to the field knower**. You would have lived through the pain experience and outgrown your personality. The mission would have been fulfilled. You would have known the field and the knower of the field. You would have become identified with the divine personality.

Divine Personality

To Unite The Field With The Knower of The Field

↓	↓

The Field   The Knower of the Field

Deep Impressions   ⟶   The Experiencer

Do a simple exercise to unite the field with the knower of the field. You can do this exercise at any point of the day. It's preferable ,however, if you do it during early morning. Make sure you do it every day for fifteen minutes.

Simply close your eyes and relax. Imagine that your task in this life time is over and you have to depart. You've done everything to the best of your abilities.

There were a few things you could have done differently but you tried your best. Now it's time to leave. You have to let go off all the baggage ,both the pleasurable and the painful. Leaving everything aside further imagine yourself walking alone on the shores of the Ganges River completely at peace with yourself. You find a spot facing the sacred river with a view of the Himalayas and you sit down and enter deep within your being.

You feel content watching the river flow.

You feel happy meditating on the shore of the Ganges.

You feel inspired enjoying the breathtaking view of the Himalayas.

You feel relieved that nothing in this world is permanent.

You feel satisfied to know that pain and suffering comes out of the stagnation of life. That which keeps flowing never suffers, and never undergoes pain.

You feel at peace with yourself by knowing that the river of purity is flowing continuously and undisturbed within you.

You feel tranquil knowing that the river of purity takes everything in its stride – pain, pleasure , ignorance and other feelings and conditions of life. Nothing is left out.

You feel fully aware that in the midst of this phenomena of events there's something within you which never suffers and which never undergoes pain.

With your eyes transfixed on the flow of the beautiful river panorama you meditate on the field within. Feeling completely serene and pristine you embrace all the deep impressions , both painful and pleasurable within you. Like a mother tightly holding on to her baby child you observe your impressions carefully- You delight in the pleasurable impression and transcend the painful ones through love and compassion. With the master craftsmanship of the field knower you untie all the knots which bind the impression to the experiencer. With the heart of the lion and the love of a thousand angels backing you, you become the impression in total; you become the experience in total. You merge into the meaning of the impression. You live through the experience of the impression. You become the divine personality. No longer is there the need for a painful experience. No longer is there a need for the problem to exist. You've mastered the law of detachment and trained your mind to overcome the flaws of attachment.

Now open your eyes and get a notepad. Write these eight secrets of mastering the yoga of detachment.

1) Detachment isn't about giving up an object, breaking a relationship , or abandoning a desire.

2) Detachment is the yoga of observing the field of impressions in my mind and giving up the need to experience these impressions through a future event.

3) When I closely observe the field of impressions in my mind I reserve the power to shorten a pain experience by becoming the agent of experience and merging into the meaning of the impression.

When I practice this yoga of merging the impression with the future experience it was intended to convey I would have mastered the law of detachment and overcome the flaw of attachment.

4) I am convinced that God is not so stupid that he wants me to be hit by a truck, be cheated by someone, or be taken advantage of by another to experience a pain which I would have at some earlier stage ignorantly inflicted on another. God is all intelligence. The field of impressions is my own doing. If I have sown the seed of a painful impression the law of karma simply unites the impression with a relevant experience.

5) The practise of the yoga of detachment sets me free from the law of karma. The law of karma operates through the vast impressions stored in my mind. When I master the yoga of uniting the impression with the experience there would no longer be a need for the law of karma to influence me. I would have become my own influence. The pain that I was supposed to experience through a future event or person would no longer be necessary for I would have become the agent of the experiencer of pain.

6) **That which many call destiny is nothing but the unseen impressions waiting to express itself as the experience.** I can change my destiny, I can stop a future painful experience if I practise the yoga of observing the field of

impressions and honestly experience the meaning of the pain it was intended to deliver.

7) Says Krishna to Arjuna: "Works bound by your own nature though defective should not be abandoned as all works are covered with flaws as fire is with smoke. Work is the cause for one seeking to scale the peak of yoga and detachment the cause for one having scaled the peak of yoga."

8) I've discovered that the yoga of detachment is the process which aims for perfection through continuous improvement. That which the ignorant term to be "work" and the means by which one gets attached through the agents of desires the wise coin "the power of detachment." **When my mind is at a lower vibration any work that I do will be influenced by desires; when my mind is at a higher vibration the agents of desires no longer rule over me**. I'm free to work when I have mastered the yoga of detachment. I'm bound by my work when I fail to appreciate the flaws of attachment.

***He who stops his activities and at the same time is still thinking about them attains to nothing, he only becomes a hypocrite. That which the ignorant do with desire for results and gain, let the wise do having mastered the yoga of detachment. --- Swami Vivekananda

****

Chapter 5

The 13 Letter Mystical Word That Can Help You Reach The Supreme

Says Krishna to Arjuna: "Fools deride me when I take human form for they are not aware of my transcendent nature."

Before I reveal the 13 letter mystical word it's important to understand the answer to some few fundamental questions relating to human potential.

1) What is it that wise beings know that you're not aware of?

2) Why do we fail to absorb some of the most beautiful messages of wise men and women?

We covered these questions in great depth in the earlier chapters but I want to relate couple of events in my life which will provide a tool to remember and act on these vital pieces of wisdom. At the age of 26 I arrived in the United States to work with a major Fortune 500 company. One of the major challenges I faced initially was concerning food. I was a vegetarian and I used to eat typical Indian food. I stayed in Pittsburgh and while there were a few Indian restaurants they weren't close to the place where I was staying. Moreover, many of these restaurants weren't open for the breakfast trade, as in India, and only opened for lunch and dinner.

So breakfast became an issue for me in US. At home

in India I never had to bother about food. My mother would serve me the tastiest food. Breakfast, lunch dinner it was all there. I had got so much used to it that I thought that wherever I go there would be someone who would take care of my food. When you get used to certain things for a long time you start taking them for granted. I loved food so I had no option but to cook my own breakfast and some other meals.

The Recipe For Failure

I was fond of okra. In India this vegetable is also called the "ladies finger." So I went to the store, bought the vegetable, and I printed out the recipe which my mother had emailed me. This is how I started my adventure of cooking. I followed every single thing written in the recipe except one thing. My mother told me to keep the fire low but I thought if I keep the fire high it will cook faster . So I kept the fire on high and I went to take a bath and when I returned I was disappointed. The okra was roasted since I had kept it on a high fire. I was so upset with myself that I couldn't understand where I went wrong. Now it's important for you to understand that I kept doing this mistake for six months even though my mother pointed out the mistake to me. I would never bother to rectify it. I would slow the fire a little and then again increase it. I was following the recipe for failure. I just couldn't understand the concept that for the food to cook properly it has to be kept on a low fire.

I continued to use the same recipe for failure in other aspects of my life too. In my career, in health matters, and in relationships. I was intelligent, and eager to do well but I lacked one thing: I failed to absorb the essence of the formula. **The "how" had become more important to me than the "why."** Thoughts, words and instructions seemed more powerful than the power of human spirit.

The Tipping Point

It was during this time that I read the works of one of a great philosopher, Ramakrishna Paramhansa. One of the most popular books written about his dictums is called *The Gospel of Ramakrishna.* This book is basically a narration of the day to day events of the master. He used to narrate simple stories to explain complex phenomena. In one of his conversations his disciple asked him

"What is the source of all power in this universe?"

Ramakrishna explained "When you turn on the fire and cook the vegetables the vegetables seem to think that they are boiling on their own. While the gas is on the vegetables keep dancing but the moment you shut down the gas the dancing of the vegetables stop. The power is all in the gas. The power is all in that one force. When we are involved in events in phenomena we tend to think that this force originates from us. This error is what keeps this universe ticking. We fail to appreciate and acknowledge the source of our power just like the vegetables which fail to appreciate the power of the gas. The intelligence of our mind is borrowed from a higher source. Know that source, respect it daily, and everything will fall in place"

The Power of Human Spirit

In the last chapter we talked about divine personality and how it's very important for you to recognise and spend time with the divine aspect of your personality. In this chapter we will talk about the characteristics of the divine personality and how it can help you absorb the essence of ancient wisdom and reveal the recipe for continuous success.

Have you ever noticed a seed? It's so tender. How about the sprout? It's so soft and yet it breaks through the sturdy and formidable earth and springs up. How could a tender seed and a soft sprout force the gigantic earth to give way? What's the secret?

Krishna revealed this secret to Arjuna. "Fools deride me when I take human form for they are not aware of my transcendent nature. Whenever virtue subsides and irreligion prevails I manifest myself again and again for the good of humanity."

Transcendence is that 13 letter word that is both mystical and often misunderstood. If you absorb the essence of this word everything else will fall in place.

All the great religious leaders were aware of this characteristic latent in every human being. We've covered the yoga of transcendence in earlier chapters so I'm not going to get into the mechanics of how to transcend. Nor do I intend to wrap a definition around transcendence. I simply want to present to you seven characteristics of transcendence which will help you absorb the essence of this mystical word and leave you with a simple exercise.

1) **The beauty of life lies in transcendence**. The ability to see, hear and feel isn't the only tool for observation and information gathering. There are far superior levels of human consciousness that aren't based on a reactionary type of thinking. When you access these channels (the four

parallel worlds) you come in direct contact with the root cause of the problem; and the levels of vibration surrounding you at this level enables you to demystify the problem.

2) There are no obstacles to transcendence. Anyone and everyone can transcend. The higher your vibration , the higher the transcendence.

3) **The will to transcend should form part of your daily habits**. Even when the whole world has shut its door to you, you're free to transcend. Always reserve quality time for transcendence.

4) Transcendence doesn't aim for perfection. It aims for improvement.

5) Elevation of thought is the key to transcendence. We don't go from error to truth. Rather we go from a lower truth to a higher truth.

6) The sky is the limit for one who has perfected the art of transcendence. There are no boundaries. The spirit keeps soaring higher and higher as you grow.

7) You are not your thoughts. You are not your circumstances. You are not your experiences. **You are as good as your ability to transcend**.

Transcendence is the single greatest skill as shown by the teachings of our most revered religious leaders. They all mastered this phenomena of transcendence. You too have the power to transcend beyond the earth, lunar and electric sphere into the world of Brahma Lok. The law of karma, the law of time , and all other laws of nature no longer bind you when you have mastered the yoga of transcendence.

Remember the example of the tender sprout and how it makes its way past the formidable earth and springs up.

Transcendence is that divine aspect of your being. Everyone can and should transcend.

Says Krishna to Arjuna: "Know that yoga to be styled which is in disjunction to the experienced-pain. This yoga is to be practiced slowly with an undejected mind."

Aim for improvement not for perfection, Krishna says. "Forward is the way to go.

Here's another useful exercise.

LIFE CHANGING EXERCISE

Imagine the following scene everyday for five minutes:

A little fish wants to flee from its enemies in the water. How does it do so? Assume that this tiny fish is going to die the next moment as a big fish is about to eat it.   What could be the last thought of the little fish? Think about some possible solutions.

...............(?)

.... (?)

THE FISH THOUGHT:

If I had known how to evolve wings and become a bird I could have flown away from the enemies in the water.

Notice carefully what the little fish thought. He said, "If I could evolve wings and become a bird I could fly. The fish didn't think that it wanted to get rid of all the big fishes surrounding it or change the immediate environment in the water. It was interested just in its own evolution.

Moral: The fish didn't change the water or the air; the change was in itself. Change is always subjective.

There are two aspects to every problem:

a) The subject which is "You."

b) The object - the environments and the circumstances limiting or confusing your options.

You can't conquer all the objective environments. You can't get rid of every person, problem, and every uncomfortable event that you encounter in your life. So what do you do?

Like the little fish you evolve wings and become a bird.

You "Take Mental Flight!"

"Knowledge is superior to repeated efforts," Krishna tells Arjuna. "Superior to knowledge is meditation. Superior to meditation is renunciation of the fruits of action. This renunciation, O Arjuna, is born out of transcendence and helps one win peace and power immediately. So by all means transcend."

"Always remember me and fight. Fixing your mind and intellect on me. Rid of all doubts you will surely attain me for you are dear to me."

The Yoga of Transcendence

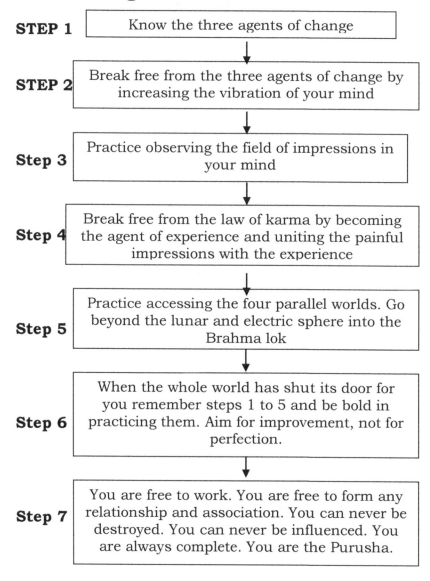

STEP 1 | Know the three agents of change

STEP 2 | Break free from the three agents of change by increasing the vibration of your mind

Step 3 | Practice observing the field of impressions in your mind

Step 4 | Break free from the law of karma by becoming the agent of experience and uniting the painful impressions with the experience

Step 5 | Practice accessing the four parallel worlds. Go beyond the lunar and electric sphere into the Brahma lok

Step 6 | When the whole world has shut its door for you remember steps 1 to 5 and be bold in practicing them. Aim for improvement, not for perfection.

Step 7 | You are free to work. You are free to form any relationship and association. You can never be destroyed. You can never be influenced. You are always complete. You are the Purusha.

Chapter 6

It is impossible that human beings can lust.

Says Krishna to Arjun "Despite his extremely wicked conduct if a man worships me exclusively he is indeed deemed worthy for his resolution is right."

Krishna says it's impossible that you can ever lust. That which triggers the attraction of the opposite sex in you is the agent of cupid. You aren't the agent of cupid. Krishna isn't too much concerned about how many times you have lusted in the past. He says it doesn't matter. The soul isn't so fragile as to be influenced by thoughts of lust. **The serenity of the ocean isn't disturbed by few erratic waves.**

Krishna simply wants you to be inspired. He wants you to find unity in your thoughts. This unity can't be found in the multitude of waves dancing in different directions. It can only be discovered when you increase the vibration of your mind and allow it to rest in the magnanimity of the ocean.

Never feel guilty, says Krishna. There's nothing like a bad thought or a bad action. There are only bad agents which represent the lower nature of Prakarti. You aren't the Prakarti. You're pure and you can never become dirty. A diamond even if it is kept years in a garbage can not lose its lustre. It will radiate the moment you uncover the dirt.

Whenever this agent of Cupid strikes you , do two things:

1) Simply remind yourself that your mind is at a low vibration.

2) Sit down in silence and increase the rate of vibration of your mind.

If you follow these two steps you'll quickly discover that you're a gigantic soul. The thoughts of lust are nothing but erratic patterns of human thinking which arises due to association with the lower agents of Prakarti.

"Driven by the force of lust and anger, filled with hypocrisy and egoism, offering nominal worship not ordained by the scriptures ... such senseless fools enfeeble the sense organs and persecute me dwelling within. Know such beings , O Arjuna to be demoniac..." declares Krishna.

Don't fool yourself to thinking that you have come into this world to enjoy the thought of lust, Krishna adds to his message. No matter how many times you convince yourself one day you will have to transcend it. If you begin early you gain a massive advantage to live an admirable life.

Says Krishna: "My heart bleeds when you associate yourself with the agent of Cupid who calls us senseless fools because the whole day we spend in worshipping him in various ways, – some through flawless work and others through love and affection."

In the end the lower agent of Cupid strikes us and we tumble. Our vibration of mind lowers and we get caught in the cycle of thought-action and result. Krishna says don't do that. Every time that this agent comes into play Krishna says to remember him. Understand that through bowing to this agent, Cupid, you're destroying the wonder of Krishna's teachings.

Who would want to destroy the splendour of Krishna's wisdom, the love of Christ's message and the simplicity of Buddha's sacrifice?

Say to yourself, : "Thou for whom the world of flowers bloom, kindly accept my few common flowers. Thou who feedest the universe kindly accept my poor offering of fruits. I do not know how to worship thee, I do not know how to pray to thee. If there is any virtue in my worship let it be thine.. Grant me only love ... love that never seeks for anything... love that never asks for anything...love...love...love

Krishna further advises "That which is poison in the beginning and nectar in the end know that to be the highest nature. That which is nectar in the beginning and poison in the end know that to be of a lower nature."

Take a note pad and write these eight sentences. Remember to read them every day.

1) It's impossible that I can ever lust.

2) It's impossible that I can ever experience guilt.

3) It's impossible that I can ever become impure.

4) There is only one sin in this world. Thinking about sin is the greatest sin.

5) I'm not my past thoughts. I'm not my past experiences. Experiences and thoughts can never create a dent to my real nature.

6) I have the freedom to dump my association with painful and guilty thoughts and embrace the greater part of my personality.

7) I will remember that every time that the agent of Cupid strikes me I would be destroying the god whom I so dearly worship.

8) Krishna wants me to be inspired and so will I be.

Chapter 7

How God created this universe.

When I read the Bhagavad Gita and reflect about how God created this universe everything else seems so superfluous. – Albert Einstein.

Says Krishna to Arjuna: "Of creation I am the beginning, the middle, and the end. The beginning of beings is unmanifest(the purusha). Their middle state is manifest. Their end too, is unmanifest. All beings at the end of a cycle repair to my lower nature and at the beginning of the next cycle I loose them forth."

Krishna says the word "creation" has often been misunderstood even by some intellectual giants. "Creation," Krishna points out, can only be understood if you master the science of self (soul) and appreciate the law of cycles.

Many people ponder when and how did the universe begin. However, Krishna says the question, ***"When did the universe begin?", is misleading***. It forces you to think that everything must have a start and end. That isn't true. Creation, Krishna teaches, isn't an addition of things, but always a projection of things which have already existed.

It's impossible to create something which didn't exist earlier in some form or the other.

Creation is a combination of two things: Something that existed earlier and isn't subject to change and something that was added subsequently and which is subject to change.

Consider an example. Take a car that was manufactured. A car is a combination of two things. The idea of the car which existed before its creation and the various parts assembled subsequently to manufacture the auto. The parts of the car are subject to change. However, the "idea of the car" -- representing human intelligence –continues to prevail even after the auto changes in various way.

Creation of Car

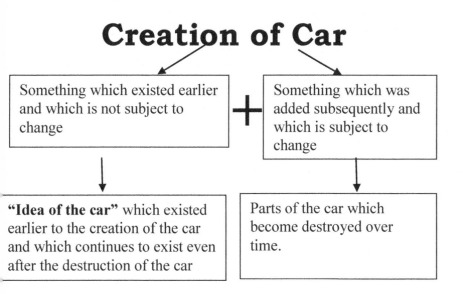

Something which existed earlier and which is not subject to change	+	Something which was added subsequently and which is subject to change
"Idea of the car" which existed earlier to the creation of the car and which continues to exist even after the destruction of the car		Parts of the car which become destroyed over time.

The goal of creation is to discovery unity. **That which existed earlier and which is not subject to change.** Anything subject to change can't be the ultimate source of creation. If you observe carefully you'll notice that even the "idea of the car" which represents intelligence of the human mind is also subject to change.

The human mind can't be the source of its own intelligence.

How do our fingers move, our legs walk, our eyes see, and our ears hear? What's the source of intelligence governing the workings of the human body?

We all know that the intelligence of the human body is *borrowed* from the intelligence of the human mind. Similarly , the intelligence of the human mind is also borrowed from something higher. Consider an example. If a lump of iron is put into the fire and made red-hot it glows and shines but its light will vanish because it's borrowed. **So decadence is possible only of that light which is borrowed and is not of its own essence.**

The human mind is vigorous at one time and weak at another because it can be acted upon by anything and everything. Therefore, the light which shines through the mind is not its own. Again, anything subject to change can't be the source of its own intelligence. Accordingly, the human mind can't be the source of its own intelligence. Its intelligence must have been *borrowed* from something else.

The "idea of the car" though it represents human intelligence is *borrowed* from something higher.

So what is the source of this infinite human intelligence?

****

Whose is it then? It must belong to that which has it as its own essence, and as such can never decay or die, never become stronger or weaker, it is self –luminous, it is luminosity itself. That which is happy has borrowed its happiness, that which has knowledge has received its knowledge and that which has a relative existence has only a reflected existence. Wherever there are qualities, these qualities have been reflected upon the substance, but "that one thing" has not knowledge, existence and blessedness as its qualities, they are the essence of "that one thing.

Swami Vivekananda

****

"Him the fire cannot burn, the water cannot wet, and wind cannot dry. That is my supreme abode reaching which none returns back."

In this passage Krishna is telling Arjuna that the Purusha is "that one thing" and the source of all creation from which everything else has manifested itself. Purusha can only be known by defining its characteristics which are superior to the intelligence of the human mind.

The characteristics of Purusha

a) If Purusha can't decay or die like the human body then it can never be destroyed. It's eternal and everlasting.

b) If Purusha can never be subject to change like the human mind it means it can't be acted upon by anything. There is no force superior to it which can influence its behavior.

c) If Purusha can't borrow its intelligence it means it should have an independent existence. It can't be the outcome of anything. It always existed. There was never a time when it didn't exist.

d) If Purusha should have an independent existence it means it can't have a relative existence. If it can't have a relative existence it means it should have an absolute existence.

It can't be that the sun has light but *it is* light. *Light isn't a quality of the sun but it is its core essence and so the light of the sun is absolute.* However, when the same light of the sun falls upon any object the light is no longer absolute in relation to that object. It becomes relative because the light is borrowed and light is seen more as a quality of that object. So wherever you see qualities in an object it has a relative existence. Everything that is created in this universe has a relative existence and perishes over time. However, Purusha is absolute and the source of all creation. It can't be that Purusha knows; *it is* knowledge. It can't be that Purusha creates; *it is* creation. It can't be Purusha is happy; *it is* happiness itself. All the qualities of happiness, knowledge, and existence found within us aren't the qualities of Purusha - they are its core essence!

Says Krishna to Arjuna: " Of the luminaries I am the sun, of the stars I am the moon, of the beasts I am the lion, of the senses I am the mind, of all beings I am the intelligence. That which is the seed of all beings I am. That which is without me, mobile or stationery, exists not, O Arjuna"

Purusha- The Source of All Intelligence

Every single thing in this universe (the sun, the moon

the stars the mountains, oceans, plants, animals and human beings) has two things in common:

1) The "idea of the object" which existed prior to the object being created.

2) That which was subsequently added to create the object.

The idea of the object represents the intelligence of the object, with Purusha itssource. This intelligence continues to exist even after the object changes or perishes. **When the sun is no longer seen at night the idea or concept of the sun continues to prevail**. When the moon isn't shining in the sky one is still aware of its existence. When the universe ceases to exist the idea of the universe continues to prevail.

Idea of the Universe

"Of those who discuss I am the dialectic."

Creation isn't an event, it's a law. In this message, Krishna explains that creation isn't something which can be discovered through research or by going back into time; rather it can be unearthed by increasing the power of your observation and understanding the law of cycles of creation.
****

All of creation follows a cycle. Take a seed, it grows into a plant and eventually into a gigantic tree. And then it dies leaving only the seed. It completes the circle- it comes out of the seed, becomes the tree and then ends as the seed again. Take the raindrop drawn in the form of vapour from the ocean, then changed into water and finally converted into vapour again. Take the huge mountains. They're continuously being worked upon by glaciers and rivers which are slowly but surely pounding them into sand. This sand then drifts away into the ocean where it settles down on its bed layer after layer, becoming hard as rocks once more to be heaped into mountains of a future generation. Again they will be pounded and pulverized and the course goes on. From the sand will rise these mountains and unto sand they go and so on. Take animal life. Look at the bird, and how it springs from the egg, lives its life, and then dies, leaving other seeds of future birds.

As with animals, so with human life.

Swami Vivekananda

■■■

"All beings at the end of a cycle repair to my lower nature and at the beginning of next cycle I loose them forth."

Krishna says time is cyclical, not linear. The word *beginning* simply means the beginning of a cycle of creation. It doesn't mean the beginning of the whole cosmos. It's impossible that creation could have a beginning. It only appears to have a beginning through the aspect of time mounted on nature. Wherever the word beginning of creation is mentioned it means the beginning of a cycle of creation. In every cycle of creation there's a beginning and an end. The end is the cause for the new beginning and the beginning is the cause for a new end.

■■■

There was a time when everything was dark. The sun didn't exist, nor the air, sky, water, or human life – nothing existed. There was no life and there was no death. There was no night or day. Milton in his great poem Paradise Lost explains this phenomenon as "No light but darkness visible." Kalidasa, the Indian poet, explains it as "Darkness which can be penetrated with a needle. It was gloom hidden in gloom. Everything was parching and sizzling. The whole creation seemed to be burning away for days when one afternoon a speck of cloud arose in one corner of the horizon. In less than half an hour it had extended over the whole earth until it was covered with cloud. Then the clouds released a tremendous deluge of rain. The cause of creation was described as will. The Purusha which existed at first had become changed into will and this will manifested itself as desire- the cosmic intelligence (Prakarti).... and the whole of creation began.

Swami Vivekananda

****

Everything that has a beginning must have an end. Everything that is created is subject to change and must undergo the greatest change of death or destruction. This destruction is nothing but going back to the source- the Purusha. Everything has to go back to its source. Nothing is spared under the law of time. This creation and destruction is called one life cycle of the universe.

Arjuna, though, has a question and asks Krishna: "How is this one life-cycle of the universe calculated and what happens at the end of a cycle of creation?"

Krishna replies: "Men who know about day and night hold that a day of Brahma consists of a thousand ages and that night also is of a thousand ages. At the break of day all individuals are born of the unmanifest and as night falls they are dissolved in the same unmanifest."

The intelligence which governs the aspect of time is called Brahma, Krishna explains. **One day of Brahma**

is equal to one life cycle of the universe. Krishna doesn't mention the duration of one life cycle of the universe. However, over the past thousands of years many great sages and scientists have attempted to calculate the duration of one life cycle of the universe. While there have been differences of opinion, everyone agrees about the unity involved in the cycle of creation.

Discoveries in the law of the cycle of creation

The sun is the source of all energy and all life which sustains this universe. But the sun also has a life span and it will eventually die, return to its source, and then be reborn. The life of the sun is 4.32 billion years and at the end of it the entire universe is destroyed and goes back to its source.

"I am Time imperishable, wrecking the dissolution of the universe," Krishna tells Arjuna.

The Dreaded Intelligence of Time

Time is one of the highest laws which runs this universe. But time shouldn't be looked upon as a duration or as a happening, Krishna relates. Neither should it be viewed in the context of past, present, and future. Rather time is that intelligence which causes the division of these time marking periods in your mind.

Time has two aspects- the real and the apparent.

What's real is based on the consciousness of time and that which is apparent is based on the practical applicability and division of time. That which is real is timeless and that which is apparent is limited. Purusha, when it entered into Prakarti , took the form of a jiva which stands for the individual soul present in every living being. Out of jiva manifested the Prana (the life force) which is the key to human consciousness. Human breathing which evolved out of Prana is the real aspect of time. It's the fly wheel of the whole system of human consciousness. Breathing first acts upon the lungs, the lungs upon the heart, the heart acts upon the blood circulation; this in turn acts on the brain and the brain on the mind which produces the awareness of the outside world.

Time therefore begins with human breathing, the act of inhalation and exhalation which makes us aware of all existence.

Breathing isn't restricted to the act of inhaling and exhaling. Instead, it's the ultimate medium through which the body unites with the soul. "Prana" - the life force causes the motion of the breath through two currents which passes through the brain and circulates down the sides of the spine, crossing at the base and returning to the brain. These two currents are the called "pingala" (the sun current) and the "ida" (the moon current). The first one, pingala, starts from the left hemisphere of the brain, crosses at the base of the brain to the right side of the spine, and recrosses at the base of the spine like one half of the figure eight. The other current, ida , reverses this action by starting at the right hemisphere of the brain and completes this figure eight.

These two currents are responsible for all the mind and body functions in our system. These currents flow day and night and make deposits of the great life forces at different points in our body; but most human beings are rarely conscious of them and fail to direct these divine forces to supercharge their consciousness.

Breathing is intimately connected with these two currents. The science of breathing gives a new direction to the "sun'" and "moon'" currents. It opens for them a new passage through the center of the spinal cord. This center of the spinal cord contains a very fine brilliant thread called "sushumna" which is luminous and which can be felt and seen through constant practice and concentration. This thread which begins from the base of the spine and ends at the pineal gland is the seat of all spiritual and divine power that you see manifested in any human being. That technique of breathing is the basis of supreme consciousness. One life cycle of the universe is intimately connected to breathing. Time therefore begins with human breathing which makes us aware of all existence, both bodily and divine.

How great sages and intellectual giants arrived at the calculation of one life cycle of the universe

a) One prana (act of breathing) is equal to four seconds which is the time taken to pronounce 10 long syllables.

b) Know that 720 such respirations make up one "muhurta" which is equal to 48 minutes. Muhurta is a special aspect of time which deals with the science of performing the right actions at the right time. Time isn't so much about time management as it is about understanding the science and art of perfect timing. **Time is about performing the right actions at the right time.** Three things are needed to succeed in any great venture: concentration, perseverance, and the will of god. This will of god is called the secret of perfect time.

Knowledge, human effort and perseverance can only take you so far; but it's the art of perfect timing that transcends all barriers and brings in the most notable results.

If you look around you'll notice that behind every great success are two things--- excellent positioning and timing. The former is related to human intellect and the latter to the art and science of time. All activities, no matter how important or mundane, are subject to mastering the nuances of right timing to achieve success.

c) Note that 30 such muhurtas of 48 minutes each make up one day of 24 hours, the time taken by earth to complete one full rotation around its own axis. **A day doesn't begin with dawn and end with dusk**. A day begins with one sunrise and ends with the next sunrise. Each day is divided into 30 muhurtas which is further divided into four equal parts of 7 ½ muhurtas each. The period from sunrise to noon, noon to sunset, sunset to midnight and midnight to sunrise is each made up of 7 ½ muhurtas.

The best time in a day is the 29th muhurta (the second to last muhurta before sunrise). This time begins 96 minutes before sunrise and lasts for 48 minutes.

Leaders throughout history have acknowledged this aspect of time and meditated during this holy hour. Those who meditate on their chosen deity during these 48 minutes will make swift and rapid progress in their spiritual life; they will be gifted with special ideas to help them overcome major obstacles and to manifest their true dreams. This muhurta, called the Brahma muhurta, is considered the most auspicious time to connect with the core of your being.

d) A month doesn't begin on the first and end on the

thirtieth. The term month is derived from the word "moon_eth." Each month begins on a new moon and ends with the next new moon. Each month is made up of 29.5 days which is the time taken by the moon to complete one full lunar cycle starting from new moon to full moon to the next new moon. Moon, is the embodied aspect of human mind and influences many important human activities. Each day of the month is characterized by the various phases of the moon in relation to the sun. The study of the various phases of the moon (waxing and waning) and its influence on human life is called "tithi" – the time it takes for the longitudinal angle of the sun and moon to increase by 12 per cent. There are 30 tithis in a month, and each of them contains many secrets for performing the important and daily activities of life at the right time.

e) Twelve such months of 29.5 days each make up one solar year of 354 days. Since the earth takes 365 days to complete one full circle around the sun every 2 ½ years one extra month of 28 days is added to fix days in relation to the sun. The 12 months are based on the entrance of the sun into a zodiac sign.

The great sages discovered two major motions of earth which will help us understand the signs of the zodiac and the apparent path which the sun takes through the sky.

The earth has two major motions- the rotational motion around its own axis and its orbital motion around the sun.

The first one is the reason why you see the sun move from the east to the west every day. The sun doesn't move from the east to the west but it appears to move because of the earth moving around its own axis.

The second motion of the earth is the orbital motion around the sun. The earth takes 365 days to complete one orbit around the sun. Since the sun is much nearer than the stars, this orbital motion makes the sun apparently move among the stars. Actually, this motion of the sun is due to the Earth's orbital motion around the sun, and while doing so, the sun apparently moves through different stars, depending on Earth's place in its orbit.

This apparent path among the stars during this orbit is represented by a line in the sky called the Ecliptic; and the stars through which the sun passes through in this line are called the signs of the zodiac. These constellations or stars are 12 in number and further sub-divided into 27 luminous bodies called "nakshatra." Together, these stars and nakshatras represent and influence the qualities and characteristics of human nature.

This apparent motion of the sun across the sky where it passes through these 12 constellations and nakshatras, together with the study of tithi (phases of moon) and muhurta, form the science of perfect timing which is called "panchang."

f) We saw in the third chapter that one year in the lunar sphere is equal to 360 years in the earth sphere. So 360 solar years in earth make up a divine year and 12,000 such divine years make up one "maha-yuga" (sub-cycle) = 4,320,000 solar years. The 4.32 million solar years is sub-divided into four eras of human existence characterized by the element of good and evil present during those periods.

The first period is called "Satya Yuga" -- the golden age where virtue, knowledge, honesty and love abounds. Every living being is blessed with abundance and there is peace and happiness. This period lasts for 1,728,000 solar years.

The second period is called "Treta yuga" where there is a slight decline in virtue and wicked activities slowly creeps in. This age is marked by 75 per cent virtue and 25 per cent vice activities. This period lasts for 1,296,000 solar years.

The third period is called "Dwapara yuga" where there is a marked decline in virtue. This age is characterized by 50 percent virtue and 50 percent vice activities. This period lasts for 864,000 solar years.

The fourth and the last period is called "Kali yuga" where wickedness, cheating, and immoral activities will be at its peak. The purest of men and women will be severely tested and face huge obstacles while wicked people will roam freely. This age, characterised by 90 per cent vice and 10 percent virtue, will last for 432, 000 solar years.

We're currently going through this last period of Kali yuga which began on 18th February 3102 BC. So 5112 years have elapsed and 426, 888 years remain.

One thousand such maha-yugas of 4.32 million years make up one day of Brahma which is 4.32 billion years. At the end of 4.32 billion years, which is one day of Brahma, the universe will be destroyed as the sun will cease to exist and life will come to an end.

However, says Krishna, the idea of the universe which existed at the time of destruction will become the cause of creation for the next cycle of creation and so on.

■■■

Here are values to help readers understand the elements of life cycles. One life cycle of the universe = 4.32 billion years (the age of the sun).

One prana (respiration) = four seconds
One muhurta = 720 prana = 48 minutes
30 muhurta = 24 hours
One month = 30 days
One solar year = 360 days (corrected every 2 ½ years)
One divine year in lunar sphere = 360 solar years in earth
One maha yuga = 12000 divine years = 4.32 million solar years
One day of brahma = 1000 maha yugas = 4.32 billion years= age of the sun.

Note that the age of the sun calculated by modern science is around 4.57 billion years which comes close to what Hindu sages found out 5000 years ago without the use of current technology. Current scientific research does support the existence of occasional mass extinctions in earth's history. These include the following major extinctions.

a) Ordovician/Silurian extinction event about 440 million years ago
b) Devonian extinction event about 375 million years ago
c) Triassic extinction event about 250 million years ago.

Though these dates of mass extinctions differ from 4.32 billion years it gives sufficient proof and insights into the concept of creation and destruction of a cycle of the universe.
****

"These actions bind me not," Krishna says. "I am as it were indifferent to them not being attached to them. Just as the vast expanse of air eternally subsists, moving everywhere, so all beings dwells in me but I dwell not in them."

Krishna explains that the thought "I create the universe" doesn't occur to him. The action of creation and dissolution is governed by the law of time. The law of time is an element of Prakarti. He is superior to Prakarti and the agents of Prakarti don't bind him. Essentially, he is the Purusha - the one without beginning and end.

Furthermore, Krishna points out that Purusha, the supreme self, will always exist and that the cycle of creation will forever prevail in the field of Prakarti. Therefore, Arjuna is advised to know both Purusha and Prakarti to be eternal.

"Just as the one sun illumines this entire world, so Arjuna, I, the owner of the field , illumine the entire field of creation."

Simple Technique To Know The Beginning of the Universe

Imagine that you have a desire to eat some tasty food and you decide to cook it yourself. Let's say you decided to cook a pizza. You preheat the oven and make the pizza on a pizza pan and put it in the oven for about 15 minutes. After 15 minutes your pizza is ready. You then spice it up with your favorite toppings and you're all set to enjoy the pizza.

Now take a notepad and divide the page into two. On the right hand side of the page write "The Beginning and End of Pizza" and on the left hand side write "Idea of Pizza."

Record the date and time when you started making the pizza and also note the time when you had finished eating the pizza. For the sake of an example choose a date of March 24 and any random time of the day.

Idea of Pizza | **The Beginning & End of Pizza**

Date: 24th March 2010

a) **Start of the Pizza: 10.30 am**
b) **End of the Pizza :11.15 am**

Now ask yourself this question: When you finished eating the pizza, *what really came to an end? There was no more pizza in the plate as it was inside your stomach, but there was something related to the pizza which continued to exist even after you finished eating.*

The idea of the pizza continues to exist even after the pizza ceases to exist. It's this idea that becomes the cause for a future desire in your mind to cook and eat another pizza.

Let's assume after three days you again get the desire to cook and eat a pizza. You repeat the same process and enjoy eating the pizza. Take your notepad again and record the timing when you started making the pizza and also note the time when you finished eating the pizza.

Idea of Pizza	The Beginning & End of Pizza
	Date: 27th March 2010
	a) **Start of the Pizza: 6.00 pm** b) **End of the Pizza :7.30 pm**

Now if someone asks you: When did you first starting making the pizza?

You might answer: *"The first time I made it on 24th March 2011. I started cooking it at 10.30 am and by 11.15 am I had finished eating the pizza. The second time I made it on 27th March 2011. I started cooking at 6.00 pm and finished eating it at 7.30 pm. and so on."*

Is your answer completely true? Not really.

A pizza can't be made without an idea of the pizza already existing.

This idea of the pizza existed before you started making the first pizza and continued to exist even after you had finished eating up the last pizza. The idea of the pizza never dies. It always existed. You might not have been aware of this idea before but it always existed, waiting to manifest itself. This manifestation in the form of a tasty pizza has a beginning and an end, but this beginning and end doesn't mean the start and end of the idea of the pizza. The idea of a pizza always existed and will continue to exist in the future and will become the cause and reason for more pizzas to be cooked in the future.

Now take a new page divide the page into two and write the "Idea of the universe" on the left hand side and "Beginning and End of the universe" on the right hand side.

Idea of the universe | **Beginning and End Of the Universe**

Now ask yourself the question: *"When did the universe begin?"*

We saw earlier that the word 'beginning' is misleading. It forces you to think that everything must have a start and end. But that isn't true.

Try this simple exercise. Try to create anything which never existed before. It's impossible. Everything created in this world has to exist in some fine form before.

You can't create something which didn't exist earlier.

Everything that you see created in this universe had to exist before in some form. This form is represented as Prakarti - idea of the universe from which the whole universe manifested.

The source of this "idea of the universe" is Purusha – That which existed earlier and which isn't subject to change. Prakarti is a manifestation of Purusha. Everything that is projected from Prakarti has a beginning and an end but Prakarti and Purusha are eternal. They never had a beginning and will never have an end.

The idea of the universe never had a beginning and will never have an end.

Everything that is projected from Prakarti has a beginning and an end. This beginning and end is called one life cycle of the universe. At the end of one life cycle the universe is destroyed and it returns back to its source. There it exists as the idea of the universe which becomes the cause for another projection of the universe in the form of another life cycle and so on.

Now close your eyes and meditate on that one reality- the Purusha from which everything else manifests and into which everything returns back.

A humble prayer to the creator of the universe

"Of the Vedic Meters I am the Gayatri Mantra," declares Krishna.

Get up early morning, sit cross-legged on the floor, and enjoy reciting the Gayatri Mantra.

The Gayatri Mantra
Aum Bhur Bhuvah Swah,
Tat Savitur Varenyam,
Bhargo Devasya Dheemahi ,
Dhiyo yo nah prachodayat.

Aum is the first sound which manifested out of Prakarti. Sound is the beginning of creation. Sounds become words, words become thoughts, and thoughts manifest into external objects. The sound Aum which requires the pronunciation of letters A, U and M represents the whole phenomena of sound producing and is considered the matrix of all sounds.

When you chant "Aum" you'll feel a familiar power rising from the core of your being. Enjoy and revel in this mystical sound.

The words "Bhur Bhuvah and Swah" represents the three parallel worlds of earth sphere, lunar sphere and electric sphere. When you chant "Bhur Bhuvah and Swah" imagine that you're manifesting the three worlds in succession. First you manifest the earth world, then the lunar world, and finally the electric world. Enjoy the experience of the power of creation. Feel powerful manifesting the three worlds.

The words "Tat Savitur" means that you pray to God for His blessings for everything that you intend to create in your life. You promise to remain detached from all the objects of creation.

When you chant "Bhargo Devasya Dheemahi" you give permission to yourself to meditate on the Purusha -the supreme being.

The word "Dhiyo" means intellect. As fire reduces everything to ashes you pray to God to end your ignorance and illumine your intellect. When you chant "Dhiyo yo nah prachodayat." you allow your intellect to travel beyond the mist of endless thoughts and you experience the first burst of divine illumination.

Note: It is advisable to chant Gayatri Mantra by lighting up the fire in (homa kundam) and reciting the prayers as an offering to Krishna through the medium of the god of fire.

Chapter 8

The Truth of All Religions

Those who think their religion is the best need to know that all the principles and tenets that they take pride in has in some form or another been discovered and preached millions of years before. Truth has always existed before religion.

Swami Vivekananda

"I am the thread which runs through the pearls of all religions," asserts Krishna.

The Map and The Territory

Krishna says we are always confusing the map with the territory. The Bhagavad Gita, the New Testament, The Dhammapada, The Q'oran and every other religious scripture is the map which helps one to navigate to the ultimate territory- the Purusha.

Consider an example. There are five people who want to travel from point A to point B. Each of these five people have different personalities and they are stationed at different points in the journey. Two of them are starting out in the journey, one is half through, and the last two are nearing completion. Assume that there are five good maps which can help one to navigate from point A to point B. Traveler no 1 who is starting out in the journey likes map # 1 because it's easy to navigate for a newbie. Traveler # 2 who is half way through the journey likes map # 2 because it gives him a good idea of the road ahead. Traveler # 3 who is close to completion likes map # 3 because it focuses completely on one thing- the goal. –reaching point B.

Each of the five maps are complete in itself and can help one to navigate from point A to point B. However, based on the personality of the person and the point where one is on the journey, one map might prove to be better than the other. The various religious scriptures are maps, complete in themselves, which can help you to reach the ultimate goal of Purusha. The superiority of one scripture over another arises because of the differences in the interpretation of the laws caused solely by the personality of the person and the point where one is on the journey.

Unity can only be found in laws and not in arrangement of words. The various scriptures only appear to be different when you pay more attention to the choice of words and less to the higher laws which these scriptures were meant to express . The law of giving, the law of life after death, the law of pure love, the law of detachment, law of the four parallel worlds, and the law of transcendence are the higher laws. Knowing and remembering these laws generates better appreciation of all religions besides bringing more personal peace and contentment.

Think about this. Would you have loved Christ if he wasn't pure and compassionate? Would you have accepted Buddha if he wasn't full of sacrifice and unselfishness? Would you have worshipped Krishna if his messages carried no wisdom and knowledge?

What came first in this universe? Love and purity or Jesus Christ? Sacrifice and unselfishness or Buddha? Wisdom and knowledge or Krishna?

Krishna was born 2000 years before Buddha who was born 500 years before Christ. The first holy scripture of the Vedas which highlighted all the higher laws was written 4000 years before Krishna was born. So what does this mean? Love always existed. Purity always existed. Sacrifice always existed. Knowledge always existed. These are the qualities of God.

God exists without form when you perceive Him in the qualities of love, purity, sacrifice and knowledge. These qualities are the embodiments of truth.

God exists with form when all its characteristics of love, power, purity, unselfishness and sacrifice are reflected on a great personality like Krishna, Buddha, Jesus, and Mohammed.

"Whosoever studies this righteous dialogue between us would have offered me a sacrifice wrought with knowledge," Krishna tells Arjuna.

When you read the *Bhagavad Gita* you realize the higher laws. When you read the other fine scriptures you realize your real nature.

There are many who think that a person can't attain perfection unless he or she has read the holy scripture of their faith. That is, however, not true, says Krishna.

The scriptures are the maps and maps are needed when you have lost your way in the journey.

However, there are few beings who don't need a map to travel. They know the journey and they know their destination.

"Whenever virtue subsides and irreligion prevails I manifest myself again and again," Krishna tells Arjuna. "Wherever thou finds a great soul trying to raise humanity know that he is born out of my splendour and that I reside in him."

All the great religious figures knew their journey and their destination. They saw the deity in themselves and encouraged people to pray to them. The choice of the words used in their preachings might appear to be different but their only motive was to help you realize the highest law - "You are the Purusha and everything else is Prakarti."

Krishna now reminds Arjuna of one of the basic elements of his advice. "Towards all beings I am the same. I hate none, nor hold anyone dear. Those who worship me with absolute devotion live in me and I in them."

Afterword

"Have you, O Arjuna, with concentrated mind listened to this? Has your confusion wrought with ignorance been dispelled?"

"God of the four worlds, Arjuna replied, "my confusion has been dispelled, and my memory of the truth has been regained by your grace. I shall do as you bid."

Arjuna then, with his mind composed and secure in his knowledge that he was pursuing the righteous path, goes on to defeat the Kauravas and achieve victory in the war.

****

Where the Yogin Krishna is, there the bowman Arjuna is ...there resides glory, victory, prosperity, and stable order.

****

Glossary

Purusha- the unmanifest, god without form, universal soul

Jiva- the individual soul

Prana – life force

Prakarti- cosmic intelligence, idea of the universe

Karma- the subtle law of cause and effect

Panchang- the science of perfect timing

Tamasic – the agent of error

Rajasic- the agent of equal opportunity

Sattvic- the agent of oneness

Latest Bestselling Books By Sri Vishwanath

1) Give Up Your Excess Baggage -24 Simple Mind Exercises That Great Men and Women Effectively Use Every Single Day

Latest Bestselling Books By Sri Vishwanath

2) Seven Spiritual Strategies – How The Enlightenment Code Can Change Your Life

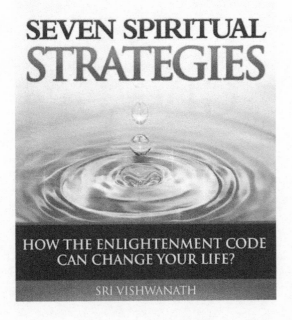

You can now experience the highest state of freedom
(without sitting in a lotus pose in a secluded cave in the Himalayas)

SEVEN SPIRITUAL STRATEGIES

HOW THE ENLIGHTENMENT CODE
CAN CHANGE YOUR LIFE?

SRI VISHWANATH

Latest Bestselling Books By Sri
Vishwanath

3) Stolen Idol

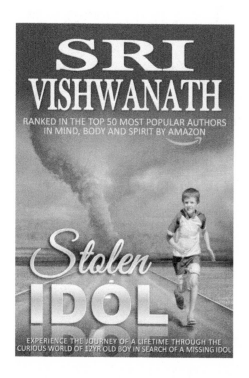

Get A Special Free Gift Worth USD 47 Right Now From Sri Vishwanath

I want to thank you for buying the book. As a special gesture I have a cool downloadable gift for you.

Simply email me right now at <u>freegift109@gmail.com</u> and we will have your special gift sent immediately to you.

Made in the USA
Monee, IL
19 December 2021

86273337R00080